Sincerely,
Stoneheart

INSIGHTS FOR A WOMAN'S HEART IN THE
SPIRIT OF *THE SCREWTAPE LETTERS*

Sincerely, Stoneheart

UNMASK THE ENEMY'S LIES,
FIND THE TRUTH THAT
SETS YOU FREE

EMILY WILSON HUSSEM

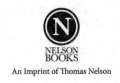

NELSON
BOOKS

An Imprint of Thomas Nelson

Sincerely, Stoneheart

Published in Nashville, Tennessee, by Nelson Books, an imprint of Thomas Nelson. Nelson Books and Thomas Nelson are registered trademarks of HarperCollins Christian Publishing, Inc.

Published in association with the literary agency of WTA Media, LLC., Franklin, Tennessee.

Author photo by Emily Wilson Hussem.

Thomas Nelson titles may be purchased in bulk for educational, business, fundraising, or sales promotional use. For information, please email SpecialMarkets@ThomasNelson.com.

Library of Congress Cataloging-in-Publication Data

Names: Wilson Hussem, Emily author
Title: Sincerely, stoneheart : unmask the enemy's lies, find the truth that sets you free : insights for a woman's heart in the spirit of the Screwtape Letters / Emily Wilson Hussem.
Description: Nashville, Tennessee : Nelson Books, [2025] | Summary: "In the spirit of C. S. Lewis's classic The Screwtape Letters, author and speaker Emily Wilson Hussem shines a light on the lies and tactics Satan uses to burden modern women with doubt, fear, insecurity, and discouragement--and empowers them with the truth that will set them free"-- Provided by publisher.
Identifiers: LCCN 2024043568 (print) | LCCN 2024043569 (ebook) | ISBN 9781400249725 trade paperback | ISBN 9781400249794 ebook
Subjects: LCSH: Catholic women--Religious life | Spiritual warfare
Classification: LCC BX2353 .W56 2025 (print) | LCC BX2353 (ebook) | DDC 248.8/43--dc23/eng/20241230
LC record available at https://lccn.loc.gov/2024043568
LC ebook record available at https://lccn.loc.gov/2024043569

Printed in the United States of America

25 26 27 28 29 LBC 5 4 3 2 1

For Pearl
Sing for joy in the shadow of His wings

Contents

CONTENTS

Contents

Introduction

Dear Reader,

When I began to write these letters, I had no intention of ever sharing them with anyone. I had read C. S. Lewis's *The Screwtape Letters* quite a few years earlier, and I was struck by the clear vision that book brought to the battle between good and evil in a person's soul.

In July 2021 I went through a personal post-pandemic awakening, and as somewhat of a prayerful expression, I started writing these letters. I felt compelled to make them a self-portrait—a way for me to look into my own soul and face questions I've really wrestled with as a woman—questions about identity, faith, friendship, marriage, motherhood, and more.

As I began this journey of soul-searching, I realized how much of my life has been a battle against insecurity, discouragement, self-loathing, comparison, and fear. There were so many layers to these battles I've faced (and still face), and I wanted to get to the root of why. *Why has the battle against these things in my life been so unrelenting, so intense?* Because the enemy has been hard at work to make sure it is. Because the enemy doesn't want me to be free.

If you are unfamiliar with *The Screwtape Letters*, it's a collection of letters from a senior demon to a younger demon, which focuses on the life of one ordinary man. Throughout the letters, the senior demon reveals and outlines the many tactics of lies and deceit he utilizes to make certain the man is on a clear path toward hell.

The book unveils the spiritual reality that there are forces hard at work to keep each of us on a path away from Christ and the life of abundance He came to give us (John 10:10). Lewis readily admitted that he was not the first to come up with the idea to highlight spiritual realities in this way: "I am told that I was not the first in the field and that someone in the seventeenth century wrote letters from a devil."*

As I wrote these letters, something about unearthing the *why* in this way began to set me free. I began to understand how calculated and specific the enemy's attacks have been against me—to keep me insecure, discouraged, and downtrodden, unable to live in the glory and freedom God made me for and struggling to glorify Him with my life.

And as the writing set me free, I began to realize that although these letters were a self-portrait, they could also be for all women. Indeed, I discovered these letters are for *you*. The battles women face are often so similar, yet we seldom vulnerably share with one another about our battles—for fear of judgment

---

* C. S. Lewis, *The Screwtape Letters* (1941; repr., Simon & Schuster, 1996), 9.

or, worse yet, confused looks that tell us we really are alone in our struggle after all.

But nothing could be further from the truth. And maybe these letters will remind you of this one thing: We are in this battle together.

This book follows the same format and shares the same foundation as *The Screwtape Letters*, but in this case the focus is an ordinary woman—just like you and me. The demons are trying to take this woman down and lead her to a life of horrific emptiness, sorrow, discouragement, and separation from Christ.

The struggles you will read about in the following letters came out of my own self-reflection, and some were born out of reflection on the struggles of the thousands of women I have had the honor of walking with in ministry throughout the years. Many of the letters encompass the stories of the women I've journeyed and spoken with, wrapped into the life of one character—"the subject," as she will be referred to in the coming pages.

The subject is the woman whose life is the main focus of the training between the two demons. Much like the Patient in Lewis's story, who makes an early turn toward Christianity, the subject in this book has also chosen a path of faith in Jesus. If your journey has been anything like mine, you know that demonic messages aimed at robbing us of the peace, joy, purpose, and fulfillment of walking with Jesus do not fall silent just because we have turned toward God. If anything, the battle grows fiercer. As Screwtape tells his protégé, "There is no need to despair; hundreds of these adult converts have been reclaimed after a brief sojourn in the Enemy's camp and are now with us."* In other words, from the demons' perspective, it's always possible to drag people—even those who have turned toward the light—back into the darkness of despair.

Beyond the subject there are a few additional characters you will come to know. I want to tell you how I arrived at the name of the character you will see the most.

Stoneheart is the senior demon who is penning letters to her successor. As I reflected on the strategies of the enemy in our lives, it became unmistakably apparent that these strategies have achieved a world filled with too many women who have hearts of stone—hearts that are unfeeling, apathetic, and hardened to the core toward others and ourselves. This is the very antithesis of what God created women for.

Perhaps, if you pause to reflect on it, you feel this in your own heart . . . that your heart has become deeply hardened over the course of your life from your experiences, your choices, your circumstances, your disappointments, your failures, and more. It is the reality for many of us—Stoneheart has been hard at work in us all.

If that all seems a bit heavy—it is. Necessarily so, if we want to look seriously at the deepest parts of our hearts and lives. What you're embarking on here is not a fun read. It's not an entertaining story that will keep you on the edge of your seat. Each letter explores a facet of femininity, of a woman's

---

* Letter 2 in Lewis, *Screwtape Letters*, 22.

heart and soul. Some of them will build on one another; others will stand alone in addressing one facet of the heart, or femininity as a whole. They'll help you look introspectively at your faith in God, your choices, your perspective, your heart, your self-image, and your life.

As a self-portrait of my own life journey so far and the lives of thousands of women, some of the letters may not apply directly to your heart and life today, but they may give you insight into the lives and struggles of women you love. Hopefully they'll offer a window into the enemy's strategies in your life and the lives of all women, and equip you to recognize many of the ways you have been deceived so you can resist these schemes and live in the truth and freedom God wants for you.

I hope this book will touch you in the depths of your soul and help you see where God wants you to be free.

It may cause you to rearrange your priorities.

It may cause you to stop, think, and pray for a good long time.

It may cause you to throw your phone into the landfill (which wouldn't be such a bad thing, right?).

Perhaps a certain letter here will offer something you think about for days, months, or years to come. (One of them in particular has truly changed the way I live every day.)

If you have a daughter, this book may shape one or many conversations you have with her about the battles we face as women.

You may also read it, find it interesting, then go on your way.

But writing this book changed me, and I hope it changes your heart and affects your soul. I hope you come to realize how certain chains have been placed around your heart so carefully to keep you from glory—making you a prisoner to an empty life—and that in response to that realization, you move boldly forward, allowing God to break these chains off your heart. And I hope that in being freed, you can live in the fullness your heart seeks and the abundance for which He knit you together in your mother's womb.

In this together,

Emily

I will give you a new heart and put a new spirit in you; I will remove from you your heart of stone and give you a heart of flesh.

EZEKIEL 36:26

LETTER 1

Entangled

My dear Belphegora,

I believe the only downside of my recent opportunity to work more closely with the Chief is having to relinquish responsibility for the assigned human I've been working on since her first day on the planet. I was so enjoying watching the results of my efforts as I nudged her ever closer to a state of outright despair, but alas! I have been promoted.

I was delighted to learn that you would be the one stepping into my shoes, and I'm confident that between your sharp instincts and my guidance, you will be more than capable of completing the project I started, leading our subject as far as possible from the light. I'm looking forward to sharing my strategies and seeing you grow in your capabilities as a purveyor of misery! Allow me to begin.

Let's first rewind to one of the most pivotal annual summits ever held by the Chief. As you haven't attended a summit yet, I'll provide a little context. During annual summits, those of us who are assigned to specific human subjects gather to talk strategy and tactics for the next year. Our conferences look much like our subjects' conferences—name tags, ballrooms, bland hotel food, big screens, the whole bit, but with far more wailing and gnashing of teeth. We thrive in chaos. But make no mistake: These summits are great opportunities to hone our craft.

At this particular conference the Chief set the foundational plan for destruction of the modern era. It was titled "Distraction." This is where it all began. In the first keynote of that weekend, the Chief shared a lightbulb moment he had after years of mulling over how to rip apart the modern culture. In his careful attention to how the subjects lived, and how that has evolved for them, the Chief realized that they thrived in the presence of one another. They felt noticed, important, and cared for within focused relationships and attention from the hearts of those who surrounded them.

So, thought the Chief, how could we create a snag in the yarn of this carefully knit sweater that would eventually unravel to its total destruction? How could we make them as miserable as possible? How could we create a recipe for an overwhelming emptiness they couldn't overcome?

Distraction.

That was the ticket—a one-way ticket to misery and emptiness.

If we could distract them and move them to pay attention to things that don't actually matter—if we could divert them entirely from their feelings, from their relationships, from their families, from their emotions, from looking at one another, from living in the present—then the unraveling would begin.

That one keynote changed everything. A distracted world is a chaotic one. Look at how far we've come.

As I pass the torch of destruction over to you for the rest of the subject's life, I'll be unpacking many different ways you can lead her to misery and emptiness. Distraction continues to play a key role in your mission, and it will do so for the rest of her days. Your goal is to occupy her mind and life with distractions as much as possible.

There are many ways to accomplish this: drama with friends or family, news feeds, arguments, screens of every shape and size, empty entertainment. Your job is to stir it up—subtly, of course. Distract her at every turn with careful, unnoticeable precision.

If you execute this well, her day will be filled with distraction, opinions, and noise from beginning to end—this is the aim. Fill her mind with so many opinions that she cannot hear the voice of our Enemy.

The root of the greatest distraction for her started as an invention called the World Wide Web. Let us revisit what a web is and does: It allows a spider to catch prey. An unassuming insect flies right into the almost-invisible trap of that spider's web and becomes stuck there with a great sense of helplessness. The Web was also like an invisible trap, and these subjects were all the prey. Floating about their lives freely, they didn't understand when the Web was invented that it would encompass the globe, just waiting until they flew into it and became ensnared forever.

They thought the Web gave them power; it only made them prey. And over time developments made the Web capable of entangling the subjects not just at home but everywhere they went. Its sticky substance has now infiltrated everything.

With our subject I've worked on this quite carefully over the years, and your job is to maintain the momentum. The consequences will be dire if you do not follow my instructions carefully.

The distraction of this Web is now the world's heartbeat. Most of our subjects barely look at or speak to one another. They sit with their hands wrapped around a little rectangular device that constantly sucks them into the Web. Note this: Her hands are *almost* folded in prayer, but there's a black hole between them—a chasm that is only a few square inches physically but figuratively is a limitless abyss. Our subject hopes that what she's looking for and longing for in life is just a tap or a click or one movement of her thumb away. The reality is that she no longer knows what she's seeking, and the black hole of her screen ensures that she doesn't take time to consider it.

When you're pushing distraction through this means, see how easily you can get something on her screen to consume her thoughts for an entire day—or, better yet, ruin her day. Get her steaming over the one thing said or done by that one woman she doesn't even know. See if you can get her bickering with people, or at least reading steady streams of arguments between people on her screens. Distract her mind and heart with these things to the point of deep internal preoccupation so she's unable to focus all her heart on the heart of anyone around her.

Distraction will keep her from deep connection. She'll be frustrated internally but won't know why. Or if she does know the reason, she'll grow apathetic about changing it.

Notably, one thing many of our subjects haven't seemed to notice is the deafening noise in their lives that they cannot hear. They can't hear it because it comes through their eyes.

Many of them wonder why their thought processes seem chaotic. Distraction is a gateway to internal chaos. Many of their minds are like a grandmother's house half a century ago, where every inch is cluttered with knickknacks. Their minds are cluttered to the point that many of them, including your subject, cannot think clearly anymore—all because of that noise coming through their eyes. It isn't like going to a rock concert where one has to put earplugs in because of the pain of the noise—this noise doesn't physically hurt them. It doesn't affect their ears, but it affects their minds and their ability to live with order and clarity and attention to others.

She'll be thinking in the middle of the night about what the woman with the large following said. She'll mull over a reply to an inflammatory post for hours, get sucked into drama for days, and turn on yet another screen to whisk her away from all her troubles. The distraction of it all will change the way she operates entirely and lead her to the life of emptiness we're trying to achieve.

She's searching for something meaningful but keeps coming up with misery. When you maintain a high level of noise pouring in on her from all sides, it will be difficult for her to focus on our Enemy. It will grow steadily more challenging to hear His voice.

This has been carefully orchestrated from the beginning.

When most of the noise is silent, she won't realize how deafening it truly is.

Your predecessor,

Stoneheart

LETTER 2

Solutions

Dear Belphegora,

Before you get too much further in your efforts, I must make you aware of some important background information. Many years ago, through circumstances that were well out of my control, your subject's faith became an integral part of her life.

Faith in our Enemy was built into your subject's family life, and she participated happily and readily in that infrastructure—going to church, praying before meals, and so on. Hardly an ideal context for my efforts but certainly not an insurmountable obstacle. Even those who grow up in churchgoing families are susceptible to doubt and despair. In fact, amplifying a subject's *negative* experiences with their family or church can be a very successful strategy. With a little creativity, we can use those painful experiences to drive a wedge between the subject's heart and the Enemy.

At age fourteen, however, your subject attended a major event that shifted her concept of faith from something that was just part of her family culture to something more intentional and personal. Put simply, she truly accepted it as her own. She surrendered her life in a new way to our Enemy.

I had worked against this in every way possible, so it was awful for me to witness. I knew that because of her upbringing, it wasn't going to be easy to move her totally away from her faith. But once this event occurred, I was sent floundering. It was a miserable, bitter failure for me.

Her faith began to seep into her decisions, her relationships, and her interactions with others. I tried to prevent this as much as I could, to no avail. A fire had come alight within her, and it just could not be blown out. So I had to refocus my work to destroy her.

As you know, one of our paramount missions as the young ones grow into adulthood is encouraging rebellion. Rebellion wreaks long-lasting havoc in both their lives and the lives of the elders who care for them. To accomplish this we're instructed to tempt young ones into making as many decisions as possible that will have detrimental effects on their hearts, minds, and souls for years to come.

But as I saw our subject's faith take significant root, I realized that outright rebellion was not going to be feasible. I had to ponder the best angle to take to stifle the effects of her newfound faith—not only in her own life but also in the lives of those around her. Openheartedness to our Enemy spreads all too easily from one subject to another if we're not vigilant. What if I slowly but surely attempted to stress that the path she's chosen has made her an outsider?

I whispered to her: *Faith is uncommon. And because it's uncommon, it's weird. When you're weird, you're an outsider. When you're an outsider, you'll never feel that you belong. And how embarrassing it is to not belong!*

For a young subject this is a truly terrible prospect.

When she subscribed to her faith, she subscribed to a way of living that was extremely different from what was normal. It was actually quite abnormal, which lent itself to her natural reaction of keeping quiet about it. The young ones want to belong, and they greatly fear being viewed as weird.

This provided an avenue by which it was simple to have her become sheepish, embarrassed, and even ashamed of the life she'd chosen, and to then choose to live it fervently in private but only quietly in public.

I didn't want her telling any of her peers about her findings. We never want any of the subjects telling others about our Enemy. You must understand this straight out of the gate. We want as many as possible to stay with us in the darkness, and if we can prevent the ones who've found the light from talking about where the light can be found, we have succeeded. Light prevention is surrender prevention, which is freedom prevention.

And we never want them to be free.

As your subject moved through life, she encountered real difficulties and resistance, as they all do in their process of maturing. My directive became to hold up and magnify her faith as the reason for her difficulties. In various areas I subtly pointed to faith as the problem. When she struggled in dating and experienced rejection by male subjects, I whispered that it was because of her faith. When she wasn't allowed to participate in various activities enjoyed by her peers, I suggested that her faith was a terrible burden. If she found struggles in belonging, in being understood, in being accepted, I always made sure that in the undercurrent she thought of her faith as the main impetus of these issues.

What a thorn in her side! *Having faith is not improving your life; it's hindering you from finding a spouse. It's hindering you from having the social life others enjoy. It's a hindrance to the fullness of life you're longing for.*

We want all our subjects—every last one of them—to believe that faith is the problem, not the solution to their problems. When we convince them of that, they'll walk away. They lament how chained down they feel by this terrible faith-problem they've willingly chosen to carry, and they decide to get out from under it.

When they walk away from our Enemy, it tills amazingly fertile soil for all that I will teach you in our time together. It's productive ground for your deceptions, your temptations, and all the rest of the masterful ways in which you can lead them astray, far from the life of abundance they were created for.

But when they remain close to the Enemy—it is so, so much more difficult.

Over the years, in my careful work to keep your subject in my grip, I have had to get creative about this crucial faith issue. I have utilized apathy and indifference, stoked the flame of deep anger about the dysfunction in her church community, and tried to convince her that when things are going well, there is no need to be so dependent on Him.

As her life continues to unfold, it will be up to you to observe, with the help of all the knowledge I am going to impart upon you, where you can best keep her in our chains. You will surely need to get creative in trying to distance her from Him. Fear not, though; I don't believe this is a losing battle. The momentum I have garnered in so many areas gives me hope that with proper execution, you will be able to keep peace out of every part of her life for the duration of your assignment here. She loves our Enemy and wants to glorify Him with her life, but if we keep pressure on the areas we will be discussing at length, she won't be able to get out from under the weight of them.

Off to the races,

Stoneheart

LETTER 3

Looking for the Keys

Dear Belphegora,

As we continue on our journey together, I want to set a foundation for your understanding about the matter of identity. Identity is central to our subject's life as a human being, and we must do everything we can to manipulate and warp her comprehension of who she is. Let us begin.

Beloved—that is her truest identity, given to her freely by the Enemy. She did not have to earn it. No hoops to jump through, boxes to check, forms to fill out, or tests to take to be worthy of receiving it. Beloved is simply *who she is* in every fiber of her being, internal and external—in every last cell within her body, mind, heart, and soul.

We cannot strip her of her identity as beloved—this is upsettingly outside of our capabilities. But I assure you that with a well-crafted strategy (coupled with dogged determination), we *can* prevent her from wholeheartedly embracing and living that identity.

To better illustrate our goal regarding this core identity she possesses, imagine a scene for me, if you will. You've surely seen various subjects who are about to leave their residence with just enough cushion of time to arrive on schedule for an important appointment. They go to retrieve the keys to their vehicle only to realize the keys aren't in the usual spot. Cue panic. They begin running around the house, turning over everything in sight, digging frantically in every bag and pocket as speedily as they can, trying to remember all the places they've recently been. Distraught, running up and down the stairs, searching every last possible place, they just cannot locate them. Now they'll miss their appointment—and this is a terrible thing.

That is a picture of how the Chief has instructed us to teach our subjects about their identity. He envisioned a world of females who are distraught, panicked, and looking for an identity that seems to have been misplaced—and which they must look for in countless places: in appearances, possessions, accomplishments, titles, and more. For years our subject has been running around in this chaotic and frenzied search, but she doesn't realize the keys are actually in her back pocket.

They have been there all along. She doesn't actually have to look for them anywhere.

One of my greatest tasks since the day she was born has been to get her believing she's everything but beloved. When any of our subjects are entrenched in faith groups during their upbringing, it can be more challenging to work against what is proclaimed to them so often and loudly when they're small—about how loved they are by our Enemy. They have songs about this love that children memorize in Sunday school and at summer camp and in their homes, so it can be tricky to figure out an avenue by which we can slowly undo their belief that they are beloved—and hopefully obliterate it altogether.

With a subject like ours, the Chief has outlined one method to break down that belief. The first step is by way of qualifiers:

You are loved—*but* . . .

You are loved—*if* . . .

You are loved—*when* . . .

Our work is to destroy the period at the end of that sentence. It is not "You are loved." It must always be followed by qualifiers. You'll continue to strive in carrying on the baton of belief that she is inherently not worthy of love. She might still believe in the love she has been told of and experienced, but she'll also believe that there's an asterisk there—something has to be done to earn that love. It is attained, not received. It's there but given only when various conditions are met and maintained. She has to meet those conditions day after day, for this love could be rescinded at a moment's notice in response to her poor behavior or a monumental sin or some other shortcoming she may exhibit.

We're then left with a world full of female subjects striving unceasingly to earn love that's already theirs.

Hear this clearly—it *is* already theirs.

And yet countless subjects are frittering about in unbelief, drowning in all the identities, except "beloved," that they try to take on. A delightful sight when you look at the whole lot of them!

They cannot live out their true purpose when they're confused about who they are. They cannot carry out the unique mission given them. Most importantly, when they don't understand and embrace their identity as beloved, they cannot truly be women at rest. There's a great discord in humanity when all the females are suffering from a deep internal chaos.

In this arena we also utilize comparison with other women. Some of them will look around and conclude that being loved comes so easily to other female subjects, as easily as a knife cuts through warm butter. They see women who seem loved by so many others. *Not so with you*, you must always stress. *You're one of the unlucky few who has to work for any love you get.*

May their lives be a frantic search for belovedness as we block the realization that beloved is who they already are and who they will always be.

Gleefully we roll along,

Stoneheart

LETTER 4

Insidious Roots

To my enthusiastic trainee,

I continue to take great pride in the way your dedication to destruction continues to blossom. You're a natural! Dare I say, at the risk of you growing too arrogant, you are thriving! This grows more apparent as we press on. With the speed at which you're learning, your subject's life may soon become emptier than ever.

Now we move on to the next lesson—productivity. It may sound a bit silly, but have patience; you'll be astonished by how it works within our wider plan to move them all to a life of despair.

Many of our subjects have been sculpted and shaped toward a deep proclivity for believing that their ability to *do* is essentially who they *are*. Their identity lies in the doing. The more they do, the better they are, the more valuable they are, the more worthy they are. Oh, the emptiness!

This premium on doing has been instilled within them from a young age. When a child learns that their grades on a report card are all that matters—when they're taught vigorously and unrelentingly that their intelligence, abilities, and strengths are most evident in a collection of letters on a paper—that's when they begin to believe that what they can do is all that they are.

Notice how this ties surreptitiously into our desire to confuse our subject about who she is. I've been working on this for many years.

"You *are* your grades," so many of them were shown and told, either consciously or subconsciously. They're given a letter for everything. It's like the saying, "You are what you eat," but we tell them, "You are what you *do*." The systems try to balance it out with pitiful awards here and there for good attitudes or kindness, but when it comes down to it, they're lying—everything has become only about letters and scores and therefore about productivity.

The work to undo this in the psyche is near impossible, and in that fact we rejoice. Imagine having this wired into your entire being throughout your most impressionable years. When any of our subjects fail to excel in doing as schoolchildren, they're made to feel worthless. As we strive to counteract their understanding of their true identity, this works well in our favor. It all fits together like a puzzle, as you've surely seen true in so much of our work. Brilliant, no? All credit to the Chief.

Now, if you look at the work we've done to correlate productivity with value and worth, you'll be able to see how that takes root in many areas of our subject's life. When we talk about "taking root," understand that I'm not talking about something like the roots of a small plant but more like those of a tall tree. There was once a tree she loved in her front yard, whose roots spread under her house and got into the pipes. The havoc those roots caused was quite costly—and those are the kind of roots I'm speaking of. The deep, wide roots strong enough to break apart a cement sidewalk. That is the type of root business we're in.

Prayer is one place of highest importance where this correlation of productivity and value has seeped in. Recall that I told you to keep her from prayer at all costs; we don't want her walking in relationship with our Enemy. Surely you're now seeing how these pieces fit together. Prayer doesn't feel productive. She isn't "accomplishing" anything while praying. She has nothing to show for it. She didn't make anything. She didn't achieve anything. There's nothing externally different after spending time in prayer (save a more peaceful countenance, perhaps). There are so many things on the to-do list that she could check off and have something to show for it. Prayer is not one of them. This is good.

This incessant harping on productivity is a pillar of the world that we've fortified with careful movements. They think it's making them better; it's actually ruining them.

Cheerio,

Stoneheart

LETTER 5

Top of the Podium

My attentive pupil,

I know I'm presenting a lot to you. The complexities of the mission are many, so be sure to take time to let all this soak in. When the day of your Assessment arrives, every single movement you make now will be pored over and examined to make a final decision about your future. Move wisely.

We turn now to your subject's relationships with other women.

With careful attention over the years, I've made certain that womanhood has become a competition in her mind and heart. Our objective is—and has always been—to have her view every woman as a competitor in a race. Why? Her subconscious mind will cause her to believe that tearing other women down is the means by which she can get ahead. There are few things we love more than women tearing one another down. At all costs we want them to be against one another instead of for one another.

The seeds we plant and carefully cultivate must grow into the idea that the entire scope of life as a female is always "versus," never "together."

Here's the core of where we derive this me-versus-her mentality. We've convinced them that they should be like men. If they aren't like men, they're not good enough. (Expounding upon that will have to wait for a future correspondence.) If they cannot be like men, they should at least be better than other women—in every way, always, as if the whole of womanhood is an eternal competition. Whether she views "better" as being smarter, skinnier, wealthier, more athletic, more talented, or achieving life's milestones more speedily, we just want her trying to outdo all the women around her.

Our subject used to lead a community exercise when she was a teacher for the young ones. "The spider web activity," they called it. Upon arrival at what they call a "retreat," each subject was given the name of another subject on a piece of paper. Throughout this experience over a few days, their task was to observe their assigned subject and think about qualities they admire in that person. They were to reflect on the things they found beautiful and compelling about who the person was and what she brought to the world and to the school.

On one night of their experience, they were given the assignment to write a letter to their assigned subject and openly share all the beautiful things they recognized and honored in her. When they returned to the main room where all the attendees gathered together in openness and joy, each subject read their letter aloud to the group. After the first subject read her letter, she tossed a ball of yarn to her assigned subject, while holding on to the end. It was then that person's turn to read the letter she'd written, toss the ball of yarn to her person, and so on.

By the end of the exercise, a huge web of yarn connected them all. They each felt seen and celebrated, honored and loved. Colorful yarn spread around the room, closely linking them after their vulnerable openness and expression of love for one another. It signified a togetherness they deeply longed for. There was not even the slightest hint of me-versus-her. It was only unity and harmony.

This is exactly what our Enemy wants for them. And this is everything we've worked to destroy. Instead we've worked to cultivate an intense and merciless competitiveness and discord among them all.

They don't call envy deadly for no reason. It eats them alive! If competition and comparison are at the forefront for our subject, then in every arena she'll surely observe some other woman who appears to be doing better, and she'll grow insecure. If she's insecure, it will be easier to tempt her into judgment and gossip and myriad other sin patterns. This is the first step on the slippery slope to self-hatred. And across the board we've been putting up excellent scores in achieving intense self-hatred among women.

Gossip is the most subtle method of this tearing down I speak of. It will be music to your ears: women gossiping about one another, in person or on a keyboard, belittling each other to try to feel better about themselves. The screen programs have done a terrific job of making this seem completely normal. You'll soon see. It's a constant stream of women (and men) tearing one another down without regard for the other's dignity and heart. The females are utterly vicious to one another—and it's now called entertainment! Imagine our delight as this trend got going and never stopped. It aids us greatly in our work.

Gossip is now the most commonplace activity among them, and we thrive within it. Whether they're at the lunch table, in a dorm room, or in the office, they often can find nothing to talk about except the lives of other women. Some of them—the most insecure ones—are utterly relentless in their aim to lead every conversation into gossip and slander that targets other women. Some of them do it out of a lack of confidence and some out of boredom; most do it because they've bowed to the contest of womanhood, tearing down others to try to get ahead.

We want to see a world filled with women who hate themselves because women who hate themselves have significant difficulty in truly loving one another. This self-hatred can flow into every aspect of their lives. You can see, I trust, what a great obstacle this puts in their path.

So keep playing your part in cultivating competition rather than celebration. We're doing very well in the task.

With abundant affection,

Stoneheart

LETTER 6

Have It All

Dear one,

Your efforts in our mission have impressed me greatly. But never forget that the excellence you've shown straight out of the gate is only due to the cunning skills I have imparted to you. And whatever innate prowess you may possess, you are building on the foundation of my efforts with our subject. Do not ever grow so prideful that you fail to remember why your success is possible!

Now we move on to our next pillar—the pillar of dissatisfaction.

We've worked to make dissatisfaction an integral part of the world our subject lives in. It's a golden thread interwoven into culture, media, relationships, and life as a whole. When they're dissatisfied, they're already on the verge of turning toward the temporal (and away from our Enemy) to find satisfaction. Temporal sources of satisfaction are, by definition, always temporary—so the subjects must come back to them again and again, never satisfied or filled, like a skeleton drinking water. Little do they know that the fulfillment they are seeking can be found in only one place; fortunately for us, that one true source of satisfaction is not as immediately and tangibly satisfying as the coffee drive-thru line or a package delivery of a shiny new possession. The root of dissatisfaction's effectiveness is a total focus on self, which has been part of our strategic blueprint for a long while.

Every woman's heart was built with a compass, so to speak, and true north on that compass is love of others. Women can truly find themselves by making a sincere gift of their hearts to the world. The task we've been given is to flip their built-in compass upside down so each one believes that life is about how much she can *get*, not how much she can *give*.

Even as she continues to attempt to live with sincere faith, when the compass is flipped, she'll view *getting* as the ultimate road to fulfillment, and it will lead to inescapable confusion and a life spent grasping. There is a great tension within her about what she knows she was made for—love for and service to our Enemy—and what we, along with the culture, have and continue to teach her—that this life is for getting all she can.

Generosity helps them thrive, but people are generous only when they see and care for those around them. So our goal must be to push the subject toward raging, all-consuming pride and self-ishness in every area of her life. *Life is all about me, me, me*—this is what we broadcast, trumpet, ring out. This is the desired outcome.

Her screens aid us fantastically in this messaging. As I've touched on before, there are many females she can watch who are always getting new things, always pridefully and thoroughly consumed with themselves and their own lives, and they come across as quite happy. It looks like such a happy thing to get, get, get, and to focus on me, myself, and I. When she falls into this trap, there's no telling where you can lead her. When she's unable to get what she's wanting or hoping for, dissatisfaction takes vicious hold.

Dissatisfaction is a tool you can utilize in all arenas of her life—her relationships, her possessions, her home, her work, everything. Make sure she's completely exasperated while looking at her wardrobe, discouraged while looking at her living space, and overwhelmed while seeing others buying things she can't afford. Internally, this will cause her heartache; externally, it will only cause her to buy more.

When nothing's ever good enough, she'll constantly try ways to make it better. She will strive, grasp, and yearn for something different from what she has—constantly.

Can you see it now? A totally empty life!

This is the opposite of gratitude, which you must quash at all costs. A grateful heart is one that nurtures joy, and joy is the reverse of what we're working toward together. The society in which she lives has made a wildly helpful movement toward the idea that all our subjects *deserve* what they want. They are supposed to have it all. They deserve to have all their longings fulfilled, deserve to be happy, deserve to have the life they've imagined for themselves. This blends magnificently into our work with dissatisfaction.

We use this widely broadcast belief to bolster the old tale that she shouldn't have to live with unfulfilled longings in her heart. It feels horribly unfair, especially as she looks at the women around her who seem to have received everything they ever hoped and prayed for. Understand, though, that she'll always have longings within her heart—she wasn't made for this world. But step one in my work on this matter was to get her believing that all her longings *can* be fulfilled here. As she has gone about grasping and striving in this sea of dissatisfaction, she hasn't been able to quite fulfill them all. This breeds a deeper dissatisfaction and propels her toward further grasping and striving. It moves her into a space within her faith life of grasping rather than receptivity.

Receptivity is part of the core of who she is, a core that we want to counteract with this pressure to grasp relentlessly. When she's moved to believe that grasping will help her gain it all, then when our Enemy doesn't give her something she desires, she'll go out and try to get it for herself. When people treat Him like a genie rather than a good father, we rejoice. Remember: *Get, get, get. Me, me, me. Life. Is. All. About. Me.*

The Chief's day with Eve is a trusty example for us in this work. Eve was the first female to be convinced that grasping would lead to an elevated level of fulfillment and a better, more beautiful life. What a day that was; what masterful work the Chief showed us how to execute. Changed it all forever.

Understand that in your subject's striving, grasping, and yearning in the times to come, you can also put a positive spin on the whole thing. People are obsessed with and driven by dreams and goals—always striving to reach something else. Many of them are spending countless hours trying to "achieve." If you paint all that your subject wishes as a dream, this makes her selfish desires seem more positive. If she spends as much time as possible dreaming that everything in her life looked different—looked more like what everyone else has—then dissatisfaction will be the undercurrent of every single day of her existence. When she's continuously focused on grasping at something different, something that might address her deep emptiness within, she cannot be focused on Him.

She'll miss the glory all around her.

A woman who's dissatisfied with everything cannot see our Enemy in anything.

Ta-ta for now,

Stoneheart

LETTER 7

Trust Is a Currency

Belphegora,

I want to continue sharing with you about the pillar of dissatisfaction and how it has aided us in our pursuit of unyielding, pervasive misery in every corner of your subject's heart and mind. As you may be able to guess, her screens are once again your greatest resource in aiding your quest to have the roots of dissatisfaction grow ever deeper. Without question, the screens are the main reason she's dissatisfied with everything—she is constantly bombarded with images of success, beauty, and wealth that cause her to feel dissatisfied with her own situation. Comparison with others in her community follows closely behind, infecting all her relationships with envy.

You must understand that our subjects' screens have created an alternate universe where many of their minds live. A few of our colleagues have won bona fide awards for how they've programmed their subjects to focus solely on their mind-numbing devices—morning, noon, and night. They think about almost nothing else. Some of them have departed reality, transported in their minds to a different universe, and they view their lives only through the eyes of people watching and listening to them on their ridiculous little screens. They call them "followers." We came up with that term—brilliant, no? The Enemy had twelve—and we want our subjects desperately greedy to gather as many of their own as they can hold on to.

Our colleague Gertruda won an award for her work with her subject, and recently gave a symposium on her efforts. She figured out how to move this woman toward a life in which she constantly asks herself, *"What would my followers find interesting about my life?"* This question drives every moment of her day, from the time she wakes up until the time she goes to sleep. She ponders nothing else. Whatever happens between her and her husband, everything her children do, everything she buys, everything she thinks, everything she reads, everything she feels—she broadcasts it all. She never stops. Her obsession with sharing is her complete identity.

Gertruda told attendees at the symposium that she realized the main way she could move her subject toward this mindset was to utilize the "currency of trust." Trust is now a currency among our subjects, and the value they place on it is insane (in a way that's very useful to us). The more Gertruda's subject shared about herself, the more people trusted her. The more she overshared, the more people liked her. The more they trusted and liked her, the more she could convince them to buy things. The more things they bought, the more mammon she made. And she is making mammon!

We learned so much from Gertruda—her work with her subject has been utterly revolutionary, and some of our other colleagues have been able to replicate her success.

All this helps us in our efforts to cultivate dissatisfaction in our subjects. Gertruda's subject can earn in five days what your subject earns in an entire year. Yet there's some part of your subject that believes she should be able to keep up with Gertruda's subject. She wants to be able to spend like her, live like her, look like her. Gertruda's subject makes this seem easy and attainable; your subject continues to be frustrated and dissatisfied that it is not.

She will never have a life like Gertruda's subject, and she's irritated by this. She's being ruined by her sense of dissatisfaction when she compares her life to someone like Gertruda's subject, who has in turn been lured into living an empty life in desperate pursuit of more mammon! Everybody wins.

I'm seeing pervasive levels of restlessness, vexation, and edginess within your subject that I actually didn't expect. I rejoice fully in it. I bask in her restlessness. It is your duty now to continue to fan the flames of my careful attention to this matter. Don't mess it up. More soon.

Onward to emptiness,

Stoneheart

Allergic to Depth

Dear Belphegora,

Earlier I mentioned that pivotal Distraction summit. Building on its success, the Chief later held a follow-up summit called Surface. That was surely a memorable summit—registration upon arrival was a disaster, the audio kept cutting in and out the entire weekend, and there were so many fights between our colleagues that most of the free-time activities were canceled as punishment! But the Chief was able to get the core message across in the keynotes, nonetheless. These two summits have brilliantly reinforced one another in their effects.

Here's what you must understand. Depth is one of our greatest enemies. You want to keep your subject away from depth at all costs. When she was knit together by our Enemy, she was made for depth—it's a deep longing within her, I've come to find. She longs for it in relationships, in faith, in experiences, and in love. With an empty life as our goal, keeping her as far as possible from those deep longings within her is always a victory.

A large part of what was unpacked at the summit was obliteration of our subjects' ability to feel deeply. I've toiled extensively over this, so I beg you not to get lazy and not to backpedal on any of my hard-earned progress here. The main component utilized to keep your subject from deep feelings is a quickly available distraction. If an uncomfortable feeling arises, we've provided an onslaught of distractions to numb her to it for as long as she chooses.

If she's feeling upset, she will scroll.

If she's feeling hopeless, she will eat.

If she feels overwhelmed, she'll watch a show.

She'll stay stuck on the surface by these distractions, so instead of learning from and digging into uncomfortable or undesirable feelings, she'll run away and distract herself from them. She won't learn to cope. She won't learn to sort through anything, to embrace the richness and depth of the way the Enemy created her heart to depend on Him during life's ups and downs. Her days will be spent trying to numb her heart and mind. Never embracing, never sitting in the lesson of the tension—always avoidance, always distraction. Always remaining on the surface at all costs.

Her life will be spent running away.

Many of the tactics we were taught to employ at the Surface summit are designed to shorten her attention span. Depth typically requires time. Diving deeply into something, into anything—a book, a relationship, a new skill—is never instantaneous. Since everything in the culture has become instantaneous, and thoughts that cannot be communicated in less than ten seconds have become intensely boring for so many, her attention span has been whittled down to nearly nothing. She has begun to subconsciously fall prey to the mindset that a life of depth just isn't worth the time and trouble it takes, and this will also keep her on the surface of life as a whole. These developments, along with our cunning work to suck our subjects into their screens, have helped us tremendously in this arena.

Follow me closely here since this is what it all boils down to: When your subject is no longer comfortable with depth, she'll no longer be comfortable with the Enemy. An aversion to depth will develop into an aversion to Him. His vastness is the very definition of depth, and we want her to want none of it at all. It's most important that she not bring any feelings to Him—the good, the bad, or the ugly. She must not turn to the Enemy for help in sorting through them. We must keep her turned totally into herself. Remember—always running away.

In keeping things as on-the-surface and avoidant as possible, you want to discourage her from vulnerability—in relationships, in conversations, in her family. When everything is kept at surface level, there'll be a sense of frustration within her, as with all of them. They'll crave depth, but our careful work will keep them from achieving it.

The ones who push past the uncomfortable to ask deeper questions will be the ones seen as weird and intrusive. Depth is awkward, uncomfortable. We take great delight in the fact that so many of them feel awkward speaking to anyone at all anymore. They call a vast majority of their dialogue now "small talk." It's not really small but more "surface talk." They all have so much in common in the depths of who they are, but most don't know how to connect with this naturally or effortlessly. So few know how to ask any questions or begin any conversations that have meaning. They stay on the surface—right where we want them. Lonely, miserable, running away.

We'll get to vulnerability with other female subjects as we progress together here. I'm providing you with a list of our subject's past memories of betrayal, when her vulnerability and opening up to depth backfired, when it was used against her and caused her great pain. These memories, kept at the forefront, will cause her to recoil rather than open herself to the possibility of being burned again. She longs for real connection, but you want to make it impossible. I am also providing you with a list of names and photos of subjects you must keep her away from at all costs. Some of our colleagues are failing miserably at depth prevention, and if she gets close to their subjects, their great faith and comfortability with depth could make a near waste of your efforts. It makes me sick when the poor performance of our colleagues makes our job harder than it has to be, and it makes their predecessors look bad. Don't you dare think about making me look bad, you hear?

That list of memories I'll send will aid you well. In every critical moment when she might move toward depth in friendship and relationship, you'll use all these past rejections to convince her she'll only be rejected again. She'll recoil at those memories, and this will keep her from opening herself up again. It will keep her from connection; it will keep her from the depth she longs for.

This is good.

> With eyes twinkling with
> mischief,
>
> *Stancheart*

LETTER 9

The Next Time Is Never Different

Belphegora, my student,

Now, you're aware that your subject has recently become a mother. Throughout our journey together, I'll teach you much about the ways my work with her has been pointed and specific to this facet of her life, which will be so prominent in the coming years. The thing you must understand about this is that motherhood is extremely demanding. It will ask much of her, unrelentingly. The folding, the rocking, the bathing, the feeding, the cooking, the changing—the duties will never, ever stop, day or night.

Repeat after me: *This is all a burden.*

That, my dear student, is the broken record we aim to keep playing in the back of the minds of all mothers. The goal is to make it all a burden in their minds. A burden—a terrible, heavy, horrible punishment. We've programmed this messaging into the cultural tides with pinpoint precision over the years. Take a quick look around, and you'll see what I mean.

Convenience matters a great deal in their culture. Convenience is a god. In many different facets of life, they fall down in worship of this idol of convenience in an attempt to make their lives as easy as possible, looking for the easiest way to do anything and everything.

This obsession with convenience has truly impacted how they view children. Many of them have been programmed—either consciously or subconsciously—to believe that raising children (which used to be a normal part of life) is a terrible inconvenience. We've worked with merciless determination in the undercurrent to rewire them to believe this. *Children will hold you back. Children will keep you from living a full and beautiful life. Children are a burden.* A victim mentality, if you will. A simple message, but we have yet to calculate just how much it has destroyed. Time will tell the scope of collateral damage in this. We wait with anticipation to see.

Raising children, I repeat, will be no easy task for your subject (or for anyone)—it requires a constant effort from her heart, soul, and mind. Nothing can prepare a woman for its inescapability. She has been accustomed to breaks throughout her life—recess, Christmas vacation, ten-minute breaks she was required to take when she was a waitress. But as a new mother, mandatory and built-in breaks are no longer her reality—let this fuel the next part of your mission. Between broken sleep, the details, the meltdowns, and everything else, she'll look for something to help get her through. She'll look for something to cope with the difficulties that come, as they always do.

Think of it as your subject needing to draw water from a well—she'll return again and again to a source to help her get by and get through, to help her along as she labors away in her tasks. She knows she cannot do it by her own power, so convincing her that the power she needs is within some finite object, obsession, or addiction rather than her faith in Him will carry you further in the mission than you can believe.

We push the finite in order to keep them from the infinite. It's quite a simple formula, really.

When she turns to the finite, the pervasive emptiness persists. This will leave a constant sour taste in her mouth about her motherhood. Like a frowning, sour-tempered child, she must trudge through every task on the list, lamenting what she has gotten herself into and wondering why she chose this life for herself. You want her to believe that she's not raising saints for glory; she's raising people for absolutely no end whatsoever.

Helping your subject lose focus on the purpose of motherhood will be a great achievement. Every load of laundry—sour. Every prepared dinner—sour. Every long and laborious bedtime routine—sour. You want her to be sour in everything. Then you want her lying in the dark at night, her mind soaked with regret, thinking that her children, when they're old, will remember only a sour mother, a mother with no patience at the end of the day.

It's a delightful cycle. She'll resolve to do better the next day, but when the first inconvenience or snag hits, start the messaging again: *This is all a burden.*

She'll continue to turn to the finite source of temporary comfort to abate it, rather than the infinite source of fulfillment.

You'll see the way many subjects joke about alcohol as the solution. We are the ones who first proposed drinking as a helpful solution to get through the days and nights—now they've made a great joke of the whole thing. We love to get them laughing and joking about their addictions and struggles, gathering others in gleeful solidarity while so few of them realize how big their problems actually are. They even put slogans about it on shirts!

Different subjects are more easily convinced than others about what will help them to get by.

Motion pictures. Sitcoms. Sometimes they call their programs "trashy," which we find wonderfully ironic—they call it what it is! They know it's like eating out of a dumpster, but they just don't care. They have no wherewithal to see how incessant consumption of trash rewires a mind completely.

Shopping. Placing orders on the Web. It's trendy for subjects to joke about how much they spend at stores without intending to, filling their lives with useless things while overlooking what they actually need. Each time they indulge, it turns out void of fulfillment, yet they keep coming back. Again and again, with the small hope that next time will be different. The next time is never different.

The hope for each subject is that she'll never learn.

Whatever you choose to push—and so many options are available that you have space to be as creative as you wish with this—it must *all* work against the truth that your subject can draw the power and perseverance she needs from the Enemy. This goes back to our biggest imperative—*keep her from prayer.* Whatever you do—keep her from it at all costs. We do not need mothers on their knees in prayer.

It's all a horrible burden—keep that record playing. We hate joyful mothers.

Yours,

Stoneheart

LETTER 10

Hold On

Dear Belphegora,

I've noticed lately that you've been losing focus as you try to juggle the complexity I have outlined to date. If you cannot stay the course, I will need to consider speaking with the Chief about your suitability for the job in advance of your final Assessment. I have not labored all these years for you to undo all my work and lose her now. I will not allow it, so remain focused. Speaking of focus, I want to return to the tool of distraction, and how you can further use it in your subject's daily life.

Deep internal distraction, as I have taught you, is used against each and every one of them, whatever their stage of life. And you'll want to utilize this against her in her mothering as well. We've heard many say over the years that one of the greatest joys is to see life through the eyes of one's children—but you want her so distracted that she rarely even looks at her children's eyes, much less sees life through them. This will, without a doubt, set up another roadblock to joy, another boulevard to misery.

Distraction is the antithesis of *presence.*

As I'm sure you've guessed by now, your subject's screen is once again a tremendous asset in this mission. If you keep it attached to her body, "Hold on!" will be the two words her children hear from her most frequently. Every single day she'll be scrolling, reading, responding, thinking, ruminating on what she could create, consume, or say next, to the point that her children slowly but surely fall into second place. There's such a constant stream of things to read, videos to watch, fights between two strangers in a comments section to peruse—it's like a black hole she can be sucked into at a moment's notice, the drop of a hat, the snap of a finger. The Web's unrelenting pull will cause her to give her children only half as much focus (or even less) as she gives to that rectangular black void.

They won't understand why, but as the children grow, their mother staring into the digital abyss will be how they remember her when they think back to their childhood.

She'll be picking up her device every chance she gets, living in a world entirely outside her own, a slave to a piece of metal and plastic, completely distracted and unable to focus on the world she actually lives in—the remarkable life our Enemy has actually given her. The fullness of joy available to her will be wholly blocked by such constant distraction. She'll miss most everything, and only when she's older will she understand how much she has missed, how truly distracted she was. Hindsight will surely be 20/20, as they say.

But in the present moment, distraction takes her mind away from her troubles. She's able to dive into an immediate escape from what's upsetting or troubling her, to eliminate the need to process, to reflect, to consider in subconscious hopes that it will eliminate the trouble altogether. Each time she puts the screen down, the trouble remains.

Yes, we've slowly eroded our subjects' capability to process troubles with such ready distraction; and they wonder why they're so constantly perturbed!

Stay with me as we unpack this multilayered onion of destruction and deceit.

My hope as you carry on this work is that your efforts make it so that her future self will always be disappointed when reflecting back on the way she's choosing to live today, especially while her children are young. Addicted to gazing incessantly at the faces of people she doesn't even know rather than the faces of the children she loves (and who *love* her), may she look back in the years ahead with such self-loathing that it will affect the rest of her life—and theirs.

We want her to regretfully ponder such things as, *What would I have witnessed with them if I hadn't been so absorbed in mindless nothingness? How many smiles did I miss? How many more moments of joy could I have shared with them if I had broken free from my addiction? How many more times could I have looked them in the eyes and given them the gaze they so deeply longed for?*

Distracted mothers raise children starving for attention. People starving for attention are easier for us to work on. Are you beginning to see how it all fits together? If there's one takeaway for you on your mission, it's this: If you implement these things well, then although her young children won't at first understand fully what her device really is or does, they'll certainly know it's more important than they are.

Toil on,

Stoneheart

LETTER 11

A Sick Game of Telephone

To my hardworking successor,

Hang in with me now on the roller coaster I've buckled you into. If the twists and turns are hurting your neck—good. They're supposed to. We weed out the weak quickly in training, and I am still taking copious notes on your successes and failures to send to administration. We have a limited amount of time together before your Assessment, so let's get to it. We're going to rewind for a brief period and talk about our subject's youth. You'll have to follow me closely as I explain to you the foundation that has been set in her understanding and fear of her own femininity.

Our mission over the years has been to condition all our female subjects to believe that growing physically into womanhood is a fearful, horrible thing. Oh, the seeds we've sown to make what is a natural, scientific, factual progression in life something extremely taboo and too uncomfortable to be discussed!

"It's awkward!" they say. Biology isn't actually awkward, but we've worked with shrewdness to make it seem so.

In the past, sharing about human biology was a simple part of human existence. In tight-knit communities of times gone by, facts were facts. Mothers and fathers raised up their children to fully understand their lives and their roles and their bodies. There was nothing awkward about it. It was life, and life was to be explained, shared in, and spoken about. Plainly.

Not anymore. How we've toiled with relentless energy to sow seeds of confusion, trepidation, shame, and dread into the natural progression of biological maturing and the ways we speak of it—most especially in the elders passing on wisdom and knowledge to the younger ones experiencing change and growth.

Most of those elders now don't know where to begin.

To begin is awkward. *Where's the starting line? What's the first thing you say about this? Where do you go to talk about it? How does one bring it up?* They wonder about many of these things. Because of the seeds of fear sown, they're unsure how to start. Therefore many never start at all. This is where the initial goal of confusion begins.

Now, follow me closely. As young ones grow biologically, many of them aren't given a comprehensive understanding of what's happening to them as their bodies change. So they fear what is happening to them. It becomes like a confusing puzzle that the little females have to figure out piece by piece on their own, with no one to look them in their eyes and say, "I'll tell you everything openly and without hesitation. You can ask me anything, and I'll tell you the answer. Let's begin."

Many elders feel uncomfortable talking about it, so the young ones have been left to learn on their own in piecemeal ways, under the dim lights of sleepovers, in gossip at lunch tables, and now in the black abyss of their screens. They piece together the science of their femininity with something a girl said at lunch about what her older sister told her. Like a sick game of telephone, we make sure it's all pieces and confusion. She stands in fear, trying to figure it all out in her young mind, too afraid to ask questions when the avenues for asking seem so closed.

When they're confused about what's happening, they're left to guess. When they're left to guess, they remember forever how confused they felt. Confused rather than empowered. Fearful rather than knowledgeable.

When the foundation of anything is confusion over clarity, we thrive.

This is the foundation we try to set for their growth in femininity. It works on many, not all. But it works often enough to have destroyed so much of the factual ease that was common in the past as the elders raised up the young ones.

On to further biological changes. Their menstruation and their fertility go hand in hand. They live a cyclical life that needs to be explained to them when they're small. Menstruation is spoken of as an inconvenient, horrible nuisance.

If they're given any facts at all, it's usually in the classroom, in what they call "sexual education." It's left to a school nurse or teacher to explain to them that they will menstruate and what they'll need to do about it logistically. That's it. They're not taught how this cyclical aspect of their lives is the powerful reason humanity can continue on. The vast majority of them receive no explanation of why this will occur in their lives; they're simply taught that it will be horrible, and it will keep happening for a long, long time.

Imagine the fear this instills within a woman from such an early moment in her life!

Femininity is horrible—that's the setup. We work to have every single one of them believe it.

This is where we wedge in the belief that it's unfair to be a woman. We work to place the focus on the horror of menstruation—not the power of fertility. They're to feel burdened with a needless struggle that men don't face, while lacking adequate information on what it all actually means and where it fits in the design of our Enemy. It's just terrible and unfair and sad and too personal to discuss openly outside of the short presentation from the nurse.

Whew, what toil it's been to get here! We worked diligently for this, and we're reaping the benefits in spades. When we start here, each of our female subjects will fail to feel fullness in womanhood from the get-go. She's prevented from an early understanding of the biological feminine design, one that can grow deeper over time. She feels sorrowful, empty, fearful, or full of dread over a life of cyclical bleeding. It's so unfair that men don't have to go through this, so unfair that women have to suffer and their counterparts don't.

It's just not fair being a woman.

Wait until I explain how this foundation sets the stage for all that lies ahead—I think you will enjoy it tremendously.

Back to work now,

Stoneheart

LETTER 12

Spread Like Wildfire

My pet,

Every last piece of this puzzle fits together, and I want to continue to unpack how femininity has become a foe, not a friend, in the general societal understanding. This is on account of our many broadcast channels used to reach women with our schemes.

Many years ago we held a summit specifically for those with female subjects. It was called Hearts of Stone, and my, was it interesting! The Chief splurged on our accommodations for this one, and it was delightful. He said it was a worthy investment for us to be as rested as possible with sharp minds primed for learning—he didn't want any of us to miss a word, for proper execution of the ideas presented was pivotal to our mission. There was also an unlimited free coffee bar in the lobby of which I took full advantage. No sleepy attendees during the afternoon presentations at this summit!

We learned that one of the most masterful movements in our grand scheme to destroy the family was to move our subjects to believe this message: *Femininity is weakness.*

For so long, societies and cultures held up the banner that femininity was beautiful, powerful, and good. Just look at the sculptures and paintings from their past, portraying the feminine body in all its softness, women breastfeeding openly, femininity at rest. Oh, how we seethed with anger at this! The celebration and understanding of our Enemy's feminine design posed a large, abominable obstacle to our work to destroy the family. But that obstacle was overcome.

We began with the messaging I mentioned in our prior correspondence, that to grow into womanhood is a terrible inconvenience, a bitter cross to carry. We built upon this to continue to create the societal messaging that it's a weak and sorrowful thing to be a woman. The male subjects are the ones who embody strength because strength is not internal; it's solely external. A ridiculous thought, right? Even more ridiculously satisfying is how many of them we've persuaded to believe it!

Here's what follows: If it's a weak thing to be a female subject, it is *better* to be a male subject. So to be strong, one must try to be more like male subjects—a fast lane to great emptiness for them all.

When the messaging was presented that femininity is equal to weakness, many of them bought into the idea that the only way to compensate was through outward displays of aggressiveness. Slowly, carefully, we taught that aggressiveness, brashness, and competitiveness are the remedy for their weakness. Watch the ones who literally take up their banners, screaming aggressively in others' faces to get their points across and prove just how strong and capable they are. It's an overcompensation beyond what we ever could have hoped for.

In the innate design of the females is a softness of spirit, an undeniable openness, an inherent gentleness. Women embody a nurturing kindness. None of this is weakness. It is astonishingly powerful, a reflection of the Enemy Himself. But the message we have successfully trumpeted is that to be nurturing is to be weak. Softness is never strong. How *offensive* it is to be called soft!

This is where our reliable colleague, the spirit of anger, can make its way in. If one embraces the softness of the feminine spirit, this is weak. If a woman desires to nurture and raise children and to focus her life there—it is weak. Instead, they have to prove how strong they are. Like a car crusher in a junkyard, we've used this perception to quash their given nature in order to confuse and destroy their families, homes, cultures, and world. And anger has bubbled up because of it. It is mind-boggling to see how this view has spread like wildfire. All that free coffee at the summit proved to be completely worth the investment.

Understand that this is a double-edged sword we wield in the battle against the Enemy's design. Our colleagues who have been assigned to male subjects have their own summits on how to dismantle any shred of virtue in the males. Over a great deal of time, we've been able to successfully utilize a countless number of male subjects to bolster the messaging that females are indeed inferior. We've worked with fervor and indefatigable determination to convince as many males as possible that their strength gives them permission to treat females in every sinful way under the sun. Although the male's inherent nature is to protect, we've taught them to exploit. Not all of them have fallen prey to this scheme, but our task is to try to achieve a success rate of 100 percent nonetheless.

Therefore, females have plenty of reasons to be angry. And the source of every single reason is all our doing. Our tactics and destruction have made them defensive. Many of them feel they have to protect themselves, prove themselves. They rebel against who they are and how they were made. In an attempt to show just how strong they are, many of them have taken up this banner of aggressiveness and anger, which resounds across their society. Stone-hearted, angry women, fighting tooth and nail to prove themselves, living like they're in some sort of contest rather than basking in the complementarity of the Enemy's design. Few of them attempt to understand the Enemy's design in the first place.

Oh, the success of the mission put forth at the summit! Anger is such a direct and pointed antithesis of the feminine spirit. I can hardly believe the progress we've seen. In all the confusion and anger that we've set and stoked into wildfire, we've witnessed a slow and steady disappearance of the qualities that make women unique and strong in the inherent nature of their design. In all the confusion these qualities have begun to diminish one by one, fading into the distance, into the rearview mirror of their society. And we can't stop screeching with glee over it!

Building upon those first days of understanding the cyclical life women lead, the next step was to get them to believe that their fertility is a burden. Yes, you understand now, a terrible burden. Step two is to get them to believe that fertility is not just a burden but a disease of sorts—a major ingredient in the recipe of their overarching weakness. It isn't something to explore the complexities of, something to understand. It's something that must be treated, suppressed, fixed.

Follow me now in this message. We want women believing that fertility is designed not for a good purpose but for wreaking needless havoc on their lives. I fear you may not be ready for this revelation, but here's the formula we must push: Fertility is a *disease*, because motherhood is a burden and children are a punishment, not a gift. That is the message.

This is how we get them to fear the whole entire thing so that they circumvent the way they were designed. We try to stifle any knowledge about the possibilities of how their lives could be good and beautiful *because of* fertility and focus instead on the ways fertility will impinge on their hopes and dreams and plans. And because we loathe the way our subjects were made, we work with ceaseless determination to get *them* to loathe the way they were made, rather than to celebrate it.

And so the norm has become a widespread lack of understanding of both the true value and beauty and purpose of the female body and the intense power our Enemy created within it.

Imagine living an entire life in a vessel you were never taught to understand. Remember that we began with sowing intense confusion and shame in how they learn about their bodies.

May that confusion and shame carry on through the years, all the way unto death.

On and on,

Stoneheart

LETTER 13

Take It and Run With It

Dear Belphegora,

Grab a cup of tea, incline your ear, and let us proceed with our discussions about femininity as weakness.

I want to take you one step further in our discussion about depth prevention, specifically regarding the females. One of the characteristics the female subjects bring to the world is a deep sense of feeling. Their ability to feel deeply, to experience a specific level of nurturing compassion for others, to be particularly moved by something, is a bedrock of the world our Enemy created. It's an essential part of the way He has woven everything together—which is why my efforts to attack this part of the fabric of how your subject lives and moves have been both potent and pointed.

Many of our efforts within this specific area have been to convince the female subjects that it's better not to feel so deeply. We want all of them to believe that feeling deeply is silly and overdramatic. It makes one a sensitive person, and a sensitive person is a weak person. Feeling deeply is therefore another ingredient in the recipe of her weakness that can and should be overcome.

This is more simple math on our part that has seemed to work well enough over the years to successfully turn things backward and upside down. It's another subtle undercurrent I interjected throughout her life, especially through her youth and teenage years: *Don't be so dramatic. You can't cry right now—you'll be seen as weak! Sensitivity does not a strong female make. If you appear to feel deeply, you'll be labeled as one of the crazy ones. Such feelings are always an overreaction. Best to tuck them away and put on a brave face instead.*

In astonishing ways the feminine heart and its ability to feel deeply has major impact on culture, families, and workplaces. We've collectively tried to reduce this impact in every possible way. As we convince our subject that only dramatic women feel deeply, she'll try shifting away from who she is inherently. She has no wish to be perceived as oversensitive, crazy, or weak, so little by little (as many of them do) she'll try to stifle this fundamental part of herself. To appear stronger she'll try to feel less and less deeply as the years go on—to at least make certain that others don't see her feeling anything at all: vulnerability prevention.

This is an area of her life where we can wield statements people have made to her in the past, either innocently or with malice, and use them against her inner peace. Hear me clearly on this. Utilizing what someone said as ammunition against her peace is a large part of the way we wreak an incessant sense of agitation over her life for years.

One sentence stated, one comment made—we take it and run with it.

So many of them have been dealt such strong verbal blows in the past, which we fully exploit to our advantage. Understand that all it takes is one person labeling her crazy in her youth and she believes it for a lifetime. Sometimes it's a parent, sometimes a teacher, a coach, or someone else she looked up to.

In discussions with my colleagues, one common thread I've found them utilizing is past comments made by male subjects to female subjects about their depth of feeling being immature and ridiculous, in need of being scaled back or eliminated altogether. So many males have no clear understanding of femininity, which is complex and often confusing. The emotional nature of the female heart can be overwhelming for them. This bolsters our work by further prompting females to shut down this part of their heart. *Calm down, you're overreacting. Why are you so sensitive? Stop being so emotional, so crazy.* I've used all of those lines to shut our subject down slowly but surely.

She has been taught little by little that her depth of feeling is just too much. When she feels deeply, it overwhelms others. So she scales it back to change who she is—to alter the makeup of her heart.

To continually shift her away from her nature in all things is paramount. It wreaks havoc on both the mind and heart; it throws off the entire equilibrium of her DNA. My efforts to do this over these many years has cost me blood, sweat, and tears—if it is not costing you the same, know that you are doing it wrong. The Chief will notice, and you will face consequences.

Ultimately, instead of the tender hearts so carefully placed within them, we hope and work toward the goal that each of them will attain that heart of stone. It won't come easily; it requires intense tenacity. But a world full of women with hearts of stone—what could be more delightful?

I was named as an ode to this overarching goal, which is, indeed, a true honor.

With limited patience for failure,

Stoneheart

Inside the Hamptons

Belphegora,

To shake things up a bit, I want to circle back and continue our lessons about what we've been able to achieve with the help of the Web, and how your subject's propensity for jealousy leads her to a state of near despair about her life and circumstances. The spirit of envy is an easy one to trigger if you utilize what I share with you in this letter.

Let's go back to the joyful day when she signed up—the day her life changed forever.

She was with a few friends on a road trip, and they were talking about this innocent tool for connection, about how to find your friends and see what they're doing and sharing and saying. However, they weren't really saying much back then—just a few words and images here and there, showing and sharing and having fun.

Your subject didn't know then, while driving through California with her friends, but in making her decision she didn't sign up for an innocent tool for connection; she signed up for a prison—a unique type of prison that evolves every day with the intent to keep her permanently locked in.

In the not-too-distant past your subject couldn't see inside extravagant houses in the Hamptons or any other place she might view as desirable. She couldn't witness fabulous vacations or luxurious shopping trips in real time. She couldn't see how the most ridiculously wealthy lived unless she knew them and they invited her to come into their houses. In years past it was far more challenging to get our female subjects to seethe with envy throughout each day. But with all the work we've done, envy now occurs almost effortlessly on our part.

It is effortless because her brain has been rearranged. Her constant electronic connectivity has changed her. Unrelenting envy stoked by that connectivity has made her completely different from who she once was. Her persistent consumption of other women's seemingly amazing lives has shifted how she sees everything internally and externally. And she wonders why she isn't happy!

It's almost unbelievable to us, this ecosystem they have created within their digital portal. But our work flourishes so fantastically because of it. There are women now experiencing constant, tenacious excitement because of their addiction to the portal. There's always a new vacation, always a new package to open, always a new bag, or clothing, or shoes, always a new car, new decor (holiday or otherwise), a new renovation for the house. For some of them, this excitement never ends. It's an everyday, every-moment affair that they both consume and broadcast to the world.

Many of the subjects become addicted to what they witness on a daily basis because, by comparison, their own lives are distressingly and exhaustingly dull. They cannot afford to vacation six times a year, order new packages every day, or renovate the house at all. So they're addicted to living vicariously through others who can. They wish and hope and dream that they can live that observed (albeit false) reality, but they can't. Oh, the pervasive sorrow this stirs up—morning, noon, and night!

I suspect you're beginning to put the pieces together here.

These ones with great clout are now everywhere (remember Gertruda's subject), basking in constant luxury and apparent perfection, spending copious amounts of mammon without a thought—they set the standard. They're the top group, and the rest of the subjects fall short. The rest now see themselves as peasants with boring lives, unable to afford practically anything while the top ones can afford everything. (At least, this is what we make them think.)

And here's the most delightfully sick part, where the envy is cultivated: Subject one can afford the gigantic house and the sparkling vacations because subject two is scraping to buy things that subject one boasts about (and makes available through the business enterprises of herself and others in the well-to-do set). Through her purchases subject two supports subject one's fabulous life that she envies deeply. A wild relationship between two women who don't even know each other, don't you think? It isn't much of a symbiotic relationship. Subject one gains the greatest benefit here, it seems. Subject two receives only sadness, sin, or despair—three things we delight to see taking root—but we chain them both down in different ways. Our colleague greed has placed chains around subject one's neck that are both very sly and very heavy.

Newness is also an important factor here. It will keep dissatisfaction at the helm of your ship. As some of these subjects broadcast something new at every turn—their new possessions, developments, hair, nails, renovations—something new all the time, this causes onlooking subjects to view their own lives as painstakingly monotonous and boring. They wake up every day to the same old repetition, with nothing novel and exciting to say or show or open. This is the common experience; those wealthy enough to attain constant newness are the outliers. And yet they are all miserable in their own ways.

The common majority become apathetic to the actuality that they are, in fact, alive and well. They grow hardened to the precious truth of this gift of life by the constant annoyance they feel in comparing their static existence to the observed lives of these perceived top-tier women, women who shake things up all the time. It eats away at our subjects on a daily basis.

This is what the new world of the digital portal has handed them—and us—on a silver platter.

Our subject is deeply frustrated that a life of greater comfort and ease is disturbingly unattainable. She had once known a degree of true contentment, which is why the day she signed up for the prison she's now in was so pivotal in our success of late.

Understand that, in theory, she could choose to walk out of this prison. But she's so fascinated by what's going on inside that she's afraid she'll miss out if she leaves; she fears having nothing to witness except her own uneventful life. I have kept her from realizing that her life would seem less uneventful if she chose to see the beauty in it. Her real life would actually seem much more sunny and glorious—everything we don't want her to have. *Apathy to life*—keep that at the forefront.

In the not-so-distant past, she broke away for a while from the attachment. Some of them break away from the chains for short periods of time, but for our subject it went on longer than usual—months, unfortunately. The foothold I'd secured over the course of years quickly vanished.

When she was free from her digital leash, my control over her stream of consciousness slowly faded. My access to her train of thought and what she pondered all day was so much more limited. She was the happiest she'd been in years—and I hated every second of it. She noticed how much more present and engaged she was in everyday life. She thought more clearly, had new ideas, was bursting with creativity, and had more time to care for what she loved. I worried that she'd broken away and freed herself forever and that all my work over the years had slipped right out of my hands.

But she came back. For most of them, the shackles are just too tightly bolted, and the pull just too intense.

She could be happy. She could be free. She has that choice.

But she doesn't want to be happy. She doesn't want to be free.

Here's hoping she doesn't break away again for an even longer time, which would be so terribly detrimental to your work.

Upward, forward, and

backward all at once,

Stoneheart

LETTER 15

Grainy Sunsets

My precious one,

Every building begins with a cornerstone. For most of the buildings we craft, the true cornerstone is pride. If you can slowly but surely incline your subject's heart to pride, she'll eventually be swallowed by it—and lose all hope for a way out.

The buildings we created on our subjects' screens began with this cornerstone. This wasn't easy to spot in the beginning. They shared about their food, posted grainy pictures of sunsets, and broadcasted their trivial activities they thought were simple and fun. They made connections with one another and shared in innocent, carefree, detached ways. Slowly but surely the cornerstone began to reveal itself, yet most of them still haven't noticed.

We called these buildings "social"—but the true long-term goal was for them to be antisocial. It was all a plan to isolate the subjects as much as possible. Clever, eh?

Understand that it was all carefully calculated. The plan came to fruition right before our eyes as we worked step-by-step on the Chief's blueprint. When a certain summit called Self-Obsessed: Pay Attention to Me was held, we were all invited to imagine a world in which the long-term plan had come to pass, a world in which we steadily separated our subjects from one another by getting them to focus entirely on themselves. Absolutely nothing "social" about it! What was fun and sweet became a prideful, soul-sucking attachment.

Your subject was sucked into a life of pride as fast as a stray bobby pin into a vacuum cleaner. It's the life of me, me, me we have discussed previously.

Look at me.
Notice what I'm doing.
Listen to what I'm saying.
Read what I think.
My opinion matters so much that you must hear it.
Watch me live.
Give me attention in any way you can.

This is what she says by her unrelenting participation and posting.

Her desperation for hearts, commentary, shares, likes, and attention has completely overshadowed the fact that the *one* heart that matters—His—has already been given to her. His attention is hers—always. She's indifferent to this now; she seeks affection and attention elsewhere, and that was the goal all along.

We've made the temptation so strong within her and the others to define themselves by the hearts they get from others, and it has blinded many of them to the solace that comes in knowing they're defined by the only heart that matters.

We could never have predicted the success of it all.

So many are swallowed up by this obsession. They now find it excessively challenging to think about anyone else. The always-connected world of the digital echo chamber helps us in this strategy because the subjects don't often share their short-comings. The connection tools they've created on their devices are not designed to invite our subjects to share their true flaws—it's all about performance, thanks to the cornerstone of pride. Pride is the most efficient weapon for shutting down any openness about all the ways women are weak. Pride and vulnerability are like oil and water. Every last one of these subjects wants to appear perfect—so there's only the smallest glimmer here and there of any real struggle in what they share. It pops up fleetingly, every so often. But that which accumulates the most attention is unattainable perfection—so they all generally stay in this lane.

None of them were created to spend their days making commentary about their lives. It's like being a play-by-play commentator for a televised football game; it's *exhausting*. At a sporting event, surely it's far more enjoyable and relaxing to be a fan in the stands. She can sit back, enjoy, take it all in. Get the snacks she enjoys, chat with friends and fellow fans, cheer when she wants to, sit quietly when she wants to. No preoccupation with any sort of outward appearance because she isn't being put on camera every few minutes. No preoccupation with living in constant anticipation about which tidbit to share next, what scene to show, what story to tell.

She could live her entire life in this way—a happy witness and participant in all that is transpiring. Instead, she chooses to be the commentator, constantly preoccupied about what to say next and do next and record next just for show. She doesn't get to enjoy the game because she's constantly talking about the game.

She was created to experience her life. But with all these carefully calculated movements toward apathy and pride and everything in between, we have moved so many of them (including her) toward constant thought about how their lives could be presented to and perceived by others.

While we continue to stoke the flame of pride, we also plant a fear in each of them that if they let go and sign off, they'll miss something of supreme, life-altering importance—or, even worse, become completely irrelevant. If she signs off permanently, there's an entire world full of thrills and excitement that she'll never be part of. She'll be an outsider. She'll no longer belong. She'll miss all the announcements and current events and what's trending. She'll no longer have the mechanism that helps her escape the depth of her feelings. She will fade away into the abyss of insignificance.

It's a catch-22, you see: Out of fear of missing out on the lives of others, she's holding on to that which is causing her to miss out on her own life. This fear has pushed her over the threshold of emptiness and desperation.

Here's the icing on the cake. As she attempts to get an ever-higher random number paying attention to her, she has little bandwidth left to pay attention to things in her own life that actually matter. It's remarkable. We've made a completely meaningless pursuit mean everything to her.

In handing the torch to you, I expect that you'll have to intensify your efforts in this specific zone. The wool has certainly been pulled taut over the eyes of the vast majority of subjects, but some of them are starting to see through it—including her. She was growing apathetic to the circus of it all, which was obviously problematic for my efforts. I'm counting on you to get the foothold back. This is urgent, so your success or failure here will make up a huge percentage of your marks upon final judgment.

The more apathetic she becomes to the circus, the more difficult it will be to reel her back into it.

Marching, marching,
marching onward,

Stoneheart

LETTER 16

Boxes to Check

To my persevering student,

Comparison has played a crucial role in the pathway to misery for your subject, and today I must begin teaching you about all the ways comparison can be wielded for her sorrow and destruction. I've taught you the importance of womanhood as competition, and one of the most important endeavors we've taken on is making faith a contest among them all. We've found this to be an incredibly effective distraction from actual growth in relationship with our Enemy—and the subject's entanglement with her digital portal is, yet again, an effective aid in the cultivation of it.

Look how holy you are! Whisper this to her at every opportunity as she fixates on the faith of women around her—whether at church, in her small group, or as she stares into her screen. It's as though she's taking a test and can't keep her eyes on her own paper, looking around at everyone else's to find the "correct" answers for how to be a valiant woman of faith.

You'll thrive in this mission if she believes that the measure of her faith is how she measures up to others—and not about her own journey at all. It's a contest. We love to see women competing in faith, judging the spirituality of women around them, sizing others up, comparing and contrasting their dedication and devotion. This spirit of competition has ruined more friendships and groups of faith than we could count. Every time we can accomplish it again, we rejoice louder.

There are many different types of devotional practices available to her in faith, and you'll want to keep at the idea that it's all a to-do list. Her faith is not a relationship but only boxes to check—always. There's no love in boxes to check, and to accomplish your goal, this is what you need her faith to be. It must be totally lacking in love.

When there's no love in her faith, there's no life in her faith.

Throughout my time I've brought her to moments when she correlates this to-do list of faith with her worth. To be holy she has to do it *all*. That's what she now believes. In order to be holy she must do all that the women around her are doing, if not more. I toiled with great effort to get her to this point; now push her as hard as you can to keep it up. Torment her! Do not let me down—I do not respond well to disappointment!

Continue to foster competition in every facet of her life. Occasionally she does well at combating this, but mostly it's destroying the way she views both herself and others. Small victories add up.

Your subject's obsession with her screens is indeed a great asset in this. Much of her faith life has become a public display rather than a hidden journey; much of it now is a show—an empty, competitive, pathetic show. We take great gladness in this. So it has been easy to have her comparing her faith to the public displays of faith she often sees. As she watches, she wants to participate more in the show—and faith as an empty show is no faith at all.

As other women share about what their time of prayer looks like, and how often they pray, and what our Enemy said or did for them in response to their prayers, she'll grow discouraged. She'll think she's doing it wrong, that she must try harder and mirror exactly what the women who seem more holy are doing to get the same, if not better, results. It's not inspiration; it's competition.

For this outcome we've removed from so many minds the importance of the hiddenness of personal relationship with the Enemy. So many of them stay discouraged in thinking they're doing it wrong, or He just doesn't love them as much because He doesn't speak to them in the same way He does with others.

You want to subtly rewire her to believe there's a bar she must reach in order to be good enough to follow Him. Make her believe that countless others are reaching this bar that she cannot. Let this feeling brew. The more it brews, the more demoralized she'll become—she'll feel increasingly that it's not worth it even to try, that holiness is unattainable for her, that it's only for other women.

This is an ideal place to have her land.

The more she feels she'll never reach the bar, the sooner you can get her to give up altogether.

Tenaciously,

Stoneheart

LETTER 17

The Things He Didn't Do

Dear Belphegora,

You're doing well with fostering comparison, so now we build upon it. Let us look now to your subject's marriage. She vowed before our Enemy and a group of others to love her husband until the day she dies. With faith as the center of their mutual promise, sowing division is considerably trickier than it would otherwise be, but there are still a number of ways you can keep her struggling within her promise. Your main task is to see if you can get her to compare her marriage to the marriages of the women around her, and those she witnesses on her portable abyss. It's often the easiest road to getting her swimming in dejection and negativity. Comparison often lends itself to feelings of insufficiency, which easily leads to resentment. Ah, resentment! One of our oldest and dearest friends.

If you execute this well, as she compares and contrasts her marriage to those of others, resentment toward her husband will build. We love to see a wife who resents her husband, especially when the resentment is such an undercurrent in her heart that she doesn't even notice its appearance. Slowly but surely, inch by inch, this can overtake her heart and provide an easy avenue for destruction down the road.

You'll begin here by causing a fixation within her on the way other husbands love their wives. Each of our subjects has unique ways they express love—you'll find this true for her and her husband, as with all others. They all love differently, some more voluntarily with words, some with actions, some with gifts. It varies. Some are more public, some more private. Some husbands are far more expressive than others. Some perform extravagant displays of love; some do not. The subject's screens will aid you greatly in helping her fixate on this.

Whatever strengths other wives publicly display or allude to about their husbands, you must always cause her to see it as a deficiency in her own. It can be husbands making poetic public tributes on special occasions, like birthdays or anniversaries, or buying their wives something beautiful and unique, or publicly displaying acts of service that her own husband would never think to do. You use all this to make her conclude that everything about her life is insufficient—both within her husband and within herself. It's not good enough and never will be.

When all she sees is her husband's lack—oh, how she will lament the place where she finds herself! When she places daily focus on this, it will make her blind to her husband's strengths and the ways he's trying to love her. This is how the resentment steadily grows.

When she's focusing on what he lacks, pride will get a foothold in her heart. She'll be so focused on where he can improve that she won't take a moment to look within herself. This is good—when she has struggles in her relationships, especially in her marriage, you always want her convinced that the other person is the problem. She's not a contributor to the struggles but only the unlucky receiver of another person's deficiency. A recipe for destruction, wouldn't you say?

Understand, though, that the goal isn't just destruction in a partial sense; we're going for total collapse. We're not there yet, but every day we plod away in hope of it.

Within the vows she made on her wedding day are graces that break through all this. Do all you can to keep her from remembering those vows, those graces. You want her wasting her energy, heart, and time comparing herself with other wives because then she has no time or energy or space in her heart to invest in her own marriage. In the midst of her lamentation over her circumstances, she has no bandwidth to sit down and reflect upon her husband's strengths and remember all the reasons she chose him in the first place.

Comparison takes up a significant amount of brainpower for them all. The more cluttered her brain can become with this deceit of ours, the more she and her marriage become like clay in our hands.

Go for broke,

Stoneheart

LETTER 18

Different Now

Dear Belphegora,

Insecure wives.

It's like the title of a trendy book or program on her big screen. *Insecure Wives.*

They have more entertainment programming about wives than you think could be possible. For some reason, countless of these pathetic ones love watching wives scream all kinds of meaningless drivel. It's a whole empire. (If you don't think we've played a part in building it, you're not following me closely enough.)

Insecurity is another side of the coin you can play in marriage. Insecurity is the main ingredient in so many recipes we cook up for the destruction of these ones, yet so often they think they're the only ones affected by it. It's an affliction they face internally that has no repercussions on others—or so they believe.

The seed was subtle when planted in your subject during her youth. Growth of the seed was unhindered; it has snowballed to take over so many different facets of her heart. She's becoming like so many of them—they act, speak, and behave directly out of their insecurity in every facet of their lives. It affects everything. So many insecure wives.

Repeat this to her: *Surely, it would be better for him to have married any woman other than you.*

This is the broken record. This is the response you whisper when she falls short, when her imperfections surface, when she's exposed for who she is—which marriage inevitably does for them all. The veil is lifted in the four walls of their shared dwelling, and they're seen for who they are. They can't prepare for the transparency of it, and when it hits, it's like a train colliding with a brick wall. She is seen for who she is, and in that exposition of the deepest inner spaces and faults and flaws, you want this rooted inside her: *He'd be better off to have married anyone other than me. I'm the worst choice he could have made. He must secretly regret it.*

As more troubles arise and more obstacles come, she'll wallow ever more deeply in self-pity—self-hatred, if you can push it to that extent. She'll be moved toward hopelessness that her marriage will ever be a deeply happy one. You can get her focused on what every other woman does well and right and how every other woman looks and lives and loves—better than she does, every last one of them. Focusing on their strengths will magnify her weaknesses within her own mind even more.

As she's focused on these flaws, she will spiral into believing she's just not a good wife. Other wives are terrific at loving their husbands in all the right ways, but for some reason she just can't get the hang of it. *I'm a poor excuse for a wife; they're all better wives than I am.*

Get her thinking about all the ways she feels she has changed for the worse since the day they met. Maybe it's her weight or her wrinkles, unhealthy habits she has developed over the years, the ways her body has changed drastically since bearing children, or an internal matter of particular struggles with certain sins she didn't used to have.

He fell in love with that girl—but you're different now. Today's version of you is much harder to love.

When she looks at old photos, when she thinks of how much more carefree and joyful she used to be, how much less frazzled she was before she bore their children, in the undercurrent let it be clear:

You're so much harder now to love.

One of our subjects has spoken publicly of how she felt when her husband looked at old photos of her. She said she hated this because she felt as if her husband was cheating on her with her former self! Imagine the intricacies of getting them to be jealous not only of one another but of their past selves! It's too good to be true.

She is not and cannot be who she was on the day she and her husband first met. She is not and cannot be who she was on their wedding day. We don't want this to be a neutral fact but a touchstone of sorrow. She'll never be as young or as carefree as she was back then. She's better than she was then, but we must always prevent our subjects from recognizing this.

As you harp on her shortcomings and what she has lost in the hurricane of these years, make her suspect that because of these shortcomings, he's looking around; his gaze is wandering. Let that festering insecurity lead her to believe that he's wishing she was different, wishing she looked like she did back then, or wishing she was more like his friends' wives—so put together, gifted, thin, or whatever you find is now bothering her. Let her squirm at the company Christmas party as all his colleagues arrive with their perfectly put-together wives and he arrives with the unfortunate dud he got stuck with.

If insecurity is the drumbeat of her life's forward march, then even when he tells her he loves her more than ever, she'll believe those words are empty and meaningless, spoken only to make her feel better.

If she were to become secure in her husband's love for her, she would be free in her marriage. Your work lies in preventing this security at any cost.

Let that drumbeat of insecurity keep sounding.

Keep calm and carry on,

Stoneheart

LETTER 19
Her Ladder Next to Mine

Young one,

Timelines and turns. These go hand in hand in the Chief's master plan to thrust all of the female subjects into unceasing discouragement. Allow me to expound upon this. Are you ready? Off we go.

Timelines and turns begin with the foundational idea that there's one trajectory and one schedule on which a female subject's life should go. Allow me to paint a picture for you here.

Imagine that each female subject has a ladder standing upright before her. This is the ladder of life, a vertical path upward. Each ladder is the same height and has the same amount of rungs that represent life's milestones—graduations, careers, boyfriends, fiancés, husbands, children, pay raises, home ownership, and the list goes on.

Next, imagine that all the female subjects stand side by side in a line that circles the globe, with their ladders in front of them. Here's the crucial dynamic behind the discouragement we want each of these subjects to experience. As each year of her life passes by, she believes she should be on the exact same rung as all the other women her age. She should be in the same stage of life, having achieved all the same milestones as the women who've clocked in the same amount of years as she has.

Our messaging is that there's only one timeline, only one way it should all go. There's only one pace at which they should be climbing the ladder. How incredibly easy we have found it to implement this belief, that their lives should all look the same. So many forget that they each have a unique and unrepeatable fingerprint and lifeprint.

From their early days our subjects are told to excel in academia, get accepted into a fabulous university, build an impressive career, find a spouse, make a lot of mammon, purchase a home—to keep climbing. They're to strive not only to achieve it all but also to manage it all effortlessly. As they achieve these life milestones—as they move up the ladder—they begin to look at the women along-side them to see whether they're keeping pace or falling behind. *Look, she's higher than me,* someone may think, and this can subtly be translated into the conclusion, *She's better than me.*

We want every single one of them to believe that women who reach the higher rungs faster are simply *better.*

Within this infrastructure of discouragement, we've slyly injected the underlying idea that their lives as females are about *turns.* This has been drilled into them since their youth, when it was always about taking turns—their turn in kickball, their turn to speak, their turn when things were being shared. Turn-taking was often about fairness—we must be fair to one another, and everything must be as even as possible across the board. At a bridal shower a forlorn subject, who's discouraged beyond her wildest imagination about the way her life is panning out, may hear someone tell her, "I know your turn is definitely coming. It's only fair."

Life isn't about evenness or fairness, but as these subjects move side by side up their ladders, they can see clearly the rungs that women nearby have attained. And if other women are advancing at a faster pace—oh, how bitterly unfair it seems!

So we press our subjects to put on the straitjacket of a timeline, to be suffocated by it for all time, and to wallow in an acute sense of worthlessness if they can't keep up. That's the long and short of it. We torment them as much as we possibly can.

Follow closely here as we peel back the layers of this onion. This is of extreme importance. Beyond the craving to be "better," we want these subjects to believe that women who've moved higher are more favored by our Enemy. We've linked their position on the ladder (and how quickly it's attained) to the Enemy's goodness and love for them. Some of them fall for it; some don't. Some waver somewhere in the middle.

The more He loves you, the faster you move up the ladder. Whatever happens in their life is intertwined with their belief in His love for them. They think His love is reflected only in what He gives or doesn't give. His one and only Son wasn't enough. There must be more, and it *has* to be in the form of life blessings *now*. This is the mindset we work with dogged determination to have them adopt. So I encourage you to get the subject thinking that the Enemy will move her up according to her behavior, her surrender, her tenacious determination to check every possible box of faithfulness to show Him she's worthy of it. The plan for life is not lovingly given; she has to earn it.

This is our infrastructure of belief for them all. It's backward and upside down and sideways from how it all actually works. Stay with me on this. When they reach a milestone in life, we've done our best to rearrange their thinking toward the vision that reaching a milestone is a personal achievement, not an unfolding of the plan for them. To secure a husband is often seen as an achievement, as a trophy to hold up. All upward steps in life are achieved, not received.

Here are a few of my favorite collateral effects in their lives from our timelines-and-turns messaging.

They marry male subjects they know they shouldn't, only because they want to stick to the timeline. *Breaking up with this man now will set me back years on the timeline; I'll be behind everyone else, and I can't start over now!*

They wallow in shame and sorrow because their best friend is ahead on the timeline, and they're so far behind. *I don't know what she's doing right and I'm doing wrong, and I feel guilty because I cannot stand her for it.*

They lash out at another female subject for whom favor and blessing seems to come easy, who seems to have some secret formula for it. This brews disdain toward the person, and if it's allowed to fester, we achieve the ultimate goal of hatred between them.

Most especially, the array of ladders is a festival of shame cultivation for us. Oh, the shame when a subject doesn't reach a certain rung "on time"! It eats her up, eats her alive. It manifests itself in one of our greatest goals in their feminine hearts—bitterness. How we revel in bitterness!

This may seem trivial, but bitterness can snowball in many ways. When a subject looks around at all the other females on their respective ladders, she isn't just bitter generally about her place on her own ladder; we can carefully cook up her bitterness *toward the Enemy* for where she finds herself at this point in life. If her place on the ladder is closely linked in her mind with His love for her, and she begins to believe she's fallen behind—then who else does she have to blame but Him? It's His fault!

She won't see that He has painted a unique picture of an abundant life in billions of different ways. She will instead believe that He has favorites—those He loves more than He loves her. Those who somehow have done things more correctly or more faithfully or more to His liking. Her life of faith will be marked by bitter distrust rather than the certainty that He's making all things work together for her good.

If you properly execute this deceit over time, she'll come to believe deep in her soul that He cares about everyone except her—that He's withholding a blessing from her for any of the reasons described above, or for no good reason at all. Remember how we did exactly that with Eve? Same old story. We haven't grown tired of it, and they never seem to catch on.

This is a big one, and I've enjoyed getting to explain it to you. There is no ladder. It's all a facade—but terribly effective nonetheless. Take some time to let this marinate.

You'll hear from me again soon.

Stay curious and cunning,

Stoneheart

Red Riding Hood

Dearest Belphegora,

Today we'll discuss the topic of purpose. It's a hefty and important concept for many of the females, including your subject. They make it a big deal as they ask, *Why am I here? What's this all about? What's the meaning of my life?* Good questions—and *we* want to be the ones who answer them.

Our subjects are designed to view "purpose" as the reason they were born, how they can give glory to our Enemy, what they have to offer the world, the gifts they have to share, the difference they were uniquely created to carry out, blah blah blah.

This one is relatively straightforward in the sea of intricacies that I've already laid out for you. Our task is to diminish their purpose as much as possible in their own minds. They'll eventually become discouraged enough to give up trying to live out their purpose to any degree and, perhaps, not even bother to explore what it might be.

Here are a few of our best lines on our broadcast channels with your subject:

> *Look around at the amazing contributions of females;*
>   *you, on the other hand, have nothing to offer.*
> *There's nothing special about you.*
> *There's nothing unique or impressive about your capabilities.*
> *Most people were created to make a splash in the world;*
>   *you are a sad exception.*

Here's the foundation of our precise and careful construction: The only worthwhile purpose for a female subject is one that allows her to be *seen*. We've equated purpose with the spotlight. If you're seen and celebrated, then what great purpose you have! The one who's seen, the one who holds the microphone while others listen, the one with many followers—these are the women with great purpose, a *worthwhile* purpose. A worthy purpose is one that's public. It's one you can post about, one that people are impressed by at social gatherings.

If this is not your subject's experience, her existence, her life—then there's no purpose for her. She has nothing to share, nothing to bring to the table. Her job in the world is just to get by while others with purpose make the difference. We want her to believe that others are the important ones, the ones that matter! This will lead to a dispirited heart about why she was even born in the first place. A purposeless life is an empty life. *Ta-da!*

To so many of them, the Enemy has given a hidden purpose, not a public one, and our work is to move them toward the belief that a hidden purpose is useless. You see, the ability to accept the beauty and meaning of a hidden purpose stems from one of our most formidable foes—*humility*. I haven't touched on this yet. Smashing, destroying, and circumventing humility at all costs is a top priority for us.

Here's what follows. We hope for two specific outcomes when we begin our work within the area of purpose. We want our female subjects either to manufacture a purpose that isn't uniquely in tune with the one our Enemy gave them or to give up altogether trying to discover their purpose.

Manufactured purpose is no purpose at all, but if we can get each subject to constantly attempt to be someone she is not—oh, what this cultivates is simply outstanding! Frustration, exhaustion, dejectedness. Hopelessness, sorrow, feeling overwhelmed. It takes an incredible amount of energy for anyone to try being someone they are not! The more energy she can waste on attempting this, the more distracted she'll be from praying about what her true purpose is and letting that be revealed to her.

Our Enemy's greatest disciples are the ones who serve without concern over who's watching or listening or paying any attention at all. We loathe it when one of our subjects arrives in this place and keeps striving to remain there.

You may be able to see how this branches out to affect many of our other initiatives toward emptiness. There are many collateral effects here.

One of the branches to this tree of our work in the realm of purpose is diminishing motherhood as a real purpose. Motherhood is *very* hidden, as I've discussed with you already. Understand that not all female subjects were made to be mothers—this is not the one purpose for them all. Nor is it a purpose only for those whom our Enemy especially loves. Rather, it's one specific way—a mostly hidden way—that He asks many of them to become holy.

When the Chief set out to destroy the family, one of his major efforts was to undermine the impact that motherhood has as a purpose in the minds of the young ones: *There are so many more worthwhile things you could do with your life, so many things that are far more important—because in those things, unlike motherhood, you'll be seen and recognized.*

This is the narrative. The point of life is to accomplish something great—they're taught this by many combined outside forces (we'll get to more on this forthcoming). Accomplishments are the end goal. Motherhood then becomes just another endeavor that some take on like all the rest. It's not an effort and an undertaking that will change the course of history; there's nothing exceptional about it. It's just another thing.

Our own subject's understanding of life as service to our Enemy has challenged me significantly here. On some days I have found her joyfully offering her motherhood to Him. But on days when I have been particularly successful, I have had her doubting every second that her dedication to motherhood is enough (thanks to the past few years of some serious elbow grease on my part). I will need to see increased intensity in your endeavors in this area.

I suggest leveling up the messaging that if she chooses to dedicate herself to only being a mother, she'll be throwing it all away—all her years of education, skills, professional experience. *What a waste it would be to only raise children! That's not enough of a purpose; there has to be something additional, something more.* Clever, huh? I certainly think so. When our subjects begin listening to this messaging, they overextend themselves and chase multiple purposes—supposedly more meaningful purposes than motherhood—when, in reality, mothers have the terrifying potential to transform culture from the inside of the home out.

We've also carefully woven all these tenets into the way many of them view the roles and infrastructure of their churches, faith groups, and other collective experiences meant to advance the cause of our Enemy. We've pressed subtly the idea that the only ones with a good purpose in the church are those who are seen and heard by others. The ones who make a difference in faith groups, we assure them, are those who talk, who are known, who are publicly beloved. No wonder so many of them clamor for the jobs in the spotlight!

Oh, the havoc we have wreaked in churches all over the world through convincing them one by one to view the whole thing as a mountain to climb, a competition to get to the top. Meanwhile, they're stepping on or over other subjects as they ascend in their mad rush to be seen and noticed and acclaimed. It has been a marvelously successful endeavor. If I told you all the stories, you'd be reading this letter for years!

The hidden roles in the church are seen as meaningless and useless, bearing no fruit. We make this quite clear to them. If anything, we portray the hidden roles as mere stepping stones to the greater roles in which they'll be seen and celebrated. We want to prevent any perception whatsoever that the hidden roles are, in fact, the foundation of it all.

The positive results growing out of this work include jealousy, envy, anger, gossip, and resentment. All these can grow like weeds in a greenhouse as our subjects fail to realize what's actually happening. These sins wreak havoc on their souls and cause tumult within their churches that bolster our work in staggering ways.

Be seen or be nothing—that's what we keep trumpeting. So they clamor their way toward visibility and miss the Enemy's actual calling on their lives (which is only and always the calling to Himself).

Keep up the good work,

Stoneheart

LETTER 21

The Baking Recipe

To my dedicated apprentice,

I've been surveying your every move closely, and there are quite a few areas where improvement is needed. When we began, your ability to move subtly was impressive. But over the past few weeks, your execution has grown sloppy. Your ploys have started to become overt rather than covert, and it seems that she is onto you. In fact, she is increasing her time in prayer in response to your increasingly clumsy efforts—one of the very things I warned you *not* to let happen.

This doesn't bode well for your future at all, so take some time to reflect on how you can improve your subtlety if you want to keep the job when the time for your Assessment arrives.

We'll move on now to discuss the groups they create to move female subjects closer to our Enemy—small groups, studies they do on the Enemy's Book, and the like. I'm going to teach you how to destroy these pathetic little groups from the inside out. We've done it a thousand times over, and we'll do it a thousand times over again. While you may not be directly involved in this destruction with your subject, knowledge of our strategies aimed at dismantling community is mandatory in the course of our training.

When these groups are strong, it works too directly against our work within each of our subjects. Laboring in this department is therefore of supreme importance to the overall mission. Which is, remember, an *empty life*. We don't want them in groups, feeling the sense of fullness that comes with community. We want them alone and hollow.

To destroy a group of female subjects trying to move forward in their faith, we hold three key elements at the forefront. Think of these as ingredients in a fabulous recipe that takes serious time and effort, bringing a reward that is tremendous and worthwhile.

Insecurity, *past hurts*, and *pride*.

Three fundamental ingredients that we utilize as needed, adjusting the levels depending on the holes we find in each subject's armor, the way they operate, and the obvious weaknesses they reveal.

Pride is the easiest one—it's like the eggs in a typical baking recipe. Most recipes, to be good, must have eggs. Destruction of their groups, to be good, *must* involve pride, but it must be subtle and calculated—a slow burn. Usually this can be accomplished through one subject. That's all it takes.

When a group begins to form, we wait to see which subject within it has the highest propensity to want things done a certain way and who won't shy away from making sure it happens. We work together to find this one who thinks she always knows what's best, who thinks her ideas are always the most effective, and who views herself as the most spiritually mature. We then use this subject's pride to slowly infiltrate, undermining any sort of positive functioning of the group. When a subject's pride is exercised and seeps into whatever the group is trying to accomplish, things can slowly start to turn. It can be a springboard to their turning against one another, as other subjects push back against the prideful one, and division sets in.

Pride-induced division quickly makes way for our good friend anger. Pride can pave a path for the subjects to grow frustrated and then angry with one another. After we toil awhile, they're so angry and so hurt that the last thing they want to do is talk to each other, much less pray together! Prayer is a vulnerable exercise for them. And the last thing two people who are angry with each other want to do is be vulnerable together.

The discord the prideful one causes will often lead to the group's eventual demise, but there are times when something more will be necessary for that to happen.

The second ingredient—insecurity—is added when we harp on their fear that they don't belong. When the group gathers, a large percentage of them will suspect that all the other women sitting there and talking and sharing must feel they belong in that room; they're all comfortable being there. Meanwhile, it's important that each of us works within our subject to trigger a deep-seated belief that she's the *only one* who's uncomfortable there; she fears that perhaps this group is for everyone except her. She's the odd one out. And if you play your cards subtly enough, this will cause festering insecurity.

Insecurity can be utilized in a few other ways. Because the group gathers under the banner of faith, you can play into her insecurity that her faith isn't as deep or mature or unwavering as the faith of the others. Only she has doubts and struggles. She's the unusual one here—less educated, less experienced, less mature, or whatever message of inadequacy suits a particular subject.

You can utilize this to have her start second-guessing the value of her sharing anything at all—making her fear she'll come across as unintelligent or lacking in the depth that's so obvious in the others. She'll feel afraid to expose who she really is—to expose that she truly doesn't belong.

Pride and insecurity mixed together can usually get things going to the point that the group loses all forward momentum. With these two ingredients in the mix—and with some group members feeling confused, dismayed, out of sorts, or out of place—we can then shake up past hurts.

Many of them have been hurt in these groups before. And keeping those past hurts close to the surface is extremely important. When things begin to get tense, when discord among members arises, our subjects are quick to remember—and wallow in—the old patterns of painful emotions and negative responses.

If she has been through past hurts but is still trying to join a new group, it shows that she hopes this time will be different. We want her to think that it cannot and never will be, that she'll never find the closeness she's seeking in a group of faithful women, that it's an impossibility for female subjects to get along to the point where they could advance in their shared faith. The more effectively we can drag these kinds of groups into discord and bitterness, the better chance we have that our subjects won't get up the guts to try again with a different group on a future day.

These ingredients mixed together will lead to great discouragement. Discouragement leads to in-fighting, which leads to disbanding. Whether it fizzles out or goes out in a blaze of glory is no matter here; disbanding is disbanding, and that's priority number one. Some of them try to join another group in the future; others throw in the towel forever, never to try again. We plod away in hopes that eventually they'll all give up.

While we're here, let me give you a few more important pieces to the puzzle of destruction. First, we want the foundation of all they do in these groups to be ideas—not prayer. They can have *good* ideas even, so long as they are always thinking *instead* of praying. Always producing, never communing with the Enemy in prayer. Always more concerned with growing greater numbers rather than growing deeper faith. The weakest groups are those that don't pray at all, sensing no real benefit to it, no production value. Results of prayer can never be fully calculated or seen. When they're trying to build something and see numbers rise, it's easy to convince them that prayer adds no real value.

Second, we've moved our subjects into deep concern about the branding of their groups. Turning *ministries* into *brands*— that's one of our greatest works currently in operation. The branding has to look good. "Aesthetics," they call it. Many of them believe that their group won't be successful if the branding is weak. Ha! What they don't realize is that their foundation and concerns will get them nowhere. The more concerned they become with how the group looks, the more they stray from the group's original purpose. Gather a bunch of female subjects who are confused about what the group's purpose was in the first place—that's where you win.

When these three ingredients come together in their groups, it pushes them to a sorrow and helplessness they cannot shake. They deeply desire closeness, connection, community. But those ingredients of pride, insecurity, and past hurts just keep getting in the way! They long for the togetherness this group ought to provide for them, but they can't push past the barriers.

Some groups survive longer than others, and some have special backing and bolstering from our Enemy that can make our tactics seem entirely futile, but we persist nonetheless. It has become obvious that there are some groups that He will absolutely *not* allow to fail or disband. This would drive us to madness if we focused too much on it, so we continue working on the groups that lack such obvious and impenetrable backing.

Keep them alone to keep them empty.

From me to you,

Stoneheart

LETTER 22

Convinced by Charisma

Dear one,

Let us press on with the topic of faith. You will recall that at the beginning of training I shared how your subject's faith became an important part of her life. I will never let go of my regret over this failure on my part, which is why I need you to be extraordinarily attentive here. Minimizing the role of her faith, distracting her from it, introducing her to competing interests and desires—whatever method we use, we must prevent her from growing in her faith.

After years of drumming up every angle I could to get her moving away from the Enemy rather than toward Him, I experienced a happy turn of events: Your subject's faith began to be shaped by her digital portal. By the time I handed her over to you, the time she spent stuck in the Web had become the most important factor in how she formed her opinions, thoughts, and feelings about the topic. It kept her completely out of the Enemy's Book. Instead, she was reading bite-sized pieces or listening to short clips on her portal, and this had all but taken the place of true prayer. I had detached her so completely from seeing any benefit to prayer that she simply stopped.

Attachment to prayer is attachment *to* Him. Detachment from prayer is detachment *from* Him. Presto.

I trust that you have kept up my good work in this area. In the limitless abyss of her screens, there is a seemingly infinite number of subjects saying an infinite amount of things. I got the subject listening to as many of them as possible—but nothing that stood too obviously against the Enemy. No, I got her listening to voices that seemed to fit right in with her faith, so long as they stayed at the surface level. When she began absorbing that steady stream of noise, it kept her thinking she was being faithful and learning and growing. But our subjects can grow only so much from a steady stream of short clips. Barely, if at all.

This was always the way the Chief wanted it.

Bite-sized clips talking about faith have replaced any semblance of faith-depth for most of them. Deep, abiding faith has become so very rare.

Trite, short sentences masquerading as food for thought fill our subjects' feeds. It's a platitudinous and meaningless stream of drivel. Remember the aversion to depth I spoke of? Hand in hand. Sound bites and unimaginative thoughts get most of our subjects' attention because their attention spans have dwindled so dramatically. The succession of twenty-second clips has afforded them the psychological comfort of thinking they're growing in faith while it keeps them completely on the surface, far away from the deep areas where faith actually grows.

When we wreak havoc in their lives left and right, they wonder why they struggle to believe when the only thing they've held on to for years is short clips and platitudes about our Enemy, not the Enemy Himself.

When tragedy and suffering strike, their motive for practicing faith is revealed, and often that motive is quite empty due to our efforts. Many of them don't know Him at all. They have no depth of relationship with Him because they're too preoccupied with listening to people talk *about* Him rather than talking *to* Him. Some of those people put on a great show—oh, how our subjects love a showy "relevant" faith! It's magnetic for them.

Many followers does not a sound teacher make! But for our subjects, credibility all too easily correlates with the number of people listening.

Charisma can be so convincing. And popularity—you're believable if your number is high. This has boosted our mission beautifully. We feast when faith morphs into a type of theater meant to garner attention and acclaim.

Most of the noise is opinion based, sharing from personal interpretation of anything and everything and all proclaimed as truth. A faith based on opinions is as flimsy as cheap toilet paper. Because so many of them pray infrequently, we've slowly chipped away at any discernment about who they should be listening to. This gives us a greater chance of steering them away from sound teachers and away from the Truth.

So many of them don't know what to believe anymore, but they refuse to take the time to turn off their devices, to stop listening to the opinions, and to figure out what is true through quiet prayer and contemplation.

Many don't research for themselves. Many of them are confused, lost, and listening to subjects guiding them toward everything but the Truth. And they wonder why they feel deeply empty inside! This is *exactly* the end goal when it comes to her faith life.

As subjects share bits on faith, so many of them read some brief monologue and reply, "I needed to hear this." Then they continue on, never thinking about it again, never taking time to stop or reflect on why they needed to hear it. They move on because there are other things to get to, to see, to listen to. They're all just one movement of the thumb away from additional trite nothingness. How I love seeing our subjects' hands folded not in prayer but around that little rectangular abyss.

Still following? Allow me to continue. Take time to digest the following formula.

When it comes to the arena of faith, one of our goals is to get our subjects to place their hope and trust in another of our subjects, someone who is ultimately just as fallible as they are. Whether it's someone who makes great music or delivers fantastic sermons or leads some sort of enormous group, you want to get your subject to place her hope in people, not in the Enemy.

If this fallible person has deeply affected your subject's faith, if your subject trusts this person's expertise and example, she begins to place her hope in that person. Then, when that person falters or fails, it can derail her faith completely.

The whole formula usually plays out carefully, and we give it time—lots of time. Like a fine wine. When it becomes clear that one of our subjects has many others who've placed their hope in him or her, we patiently allow their circle of listeners to grow into a substantial group. Then, at the Chief's command, we work double overtime on that leading subject to make sure they fall— and fall hard. It's like double coverage in football—the ones that could have the most impact need an elevated concentration of energy and effort. Sometimes it works, sometimes it doesn't.

My favorite downfalls are when one of our colleagues has successfully led a trusted subject down the path of a completely double life. A life of horror and deceit and sin disguised by a mask of faith and wisdom and leadership and love of the Enemy—those situations are *tremendous* triumphs for us. The higher they're raised, the further they have to fall.

The collateral damage from the fall is immense. If executed properly, the whole lot of followers will scatter like cockroaches when a light is switched on. They flee and abandon *Him* altogether because their hope was never in Him to begin with.

We've executed this successfully with more of our subjects than I can count for you. We've destroyed more groups than could be numbered. Your own subject has watched it happen numerous times with her own eyes.

Hope is an anchor for them, and they need it to carry on in all this mess. That's why it's so important for us to get your subject to misplace her hope—a total placement of it in anything other than the One who created her.

May her hope be everywhere except in Him.

Yours,

Stoneheart

LETTER 23

It's All Up to You

Dearest successor,

How are things going in the motherhood department? Are you making sure the whole thing tastes like sour milk to her? She'll be a mother until the day she is dead, so let's dive in deeper regarding your role in the journey toward destruction here.

Let me first take you through what happens throughout the course of motherhood. In the beginning it's a physically demanding process beyond what one can explain to another in any words. The small subjects need physical care from her body nearly every moment of every day—it can be excruciating for her. She's changing diapers, rocking, feeding, bathing. She's cutting fruit, wiping poop off walls, lifting children in and out of car seats. She's hugging, brushing teeth, changing sheets laden with vomit. The physical tasks are many.

As the children grow up, the physically demanding nature of the tasks slowly subsides. She realizes mothering is not just about feeding and changing; she must actually shape a person. This person will make a contribution to society that could be quite good or quite bad. This hits some mothers more intensely than others.

The age of reason comes in full force, and that tiny subject has questions. The mental load of trying to answer all of them is intense. Big questions arise, and the answers given will shape that child's view of the earth, of people, of religion, of everything. The mother has to do laundry and answer big questions at a moment's notice. She has to manage the contents of the refrigerator and manage huge feelings.

The scope of jumping back and forth between it all, and the speed at which she's required to do it, is quite something, like a Ping-Pong ball in Olympic table tennis. Have you seen the speed at which they hit it back and forth? Astonishing.

In time the small ones begin to establish their independence. Mothers mostly witness helplessly as their children begin making all their own choices—some excellent, some good, some quite bad, some permanently life-altering in the worst ways possible. Mothers play a different role through it all, and navigating how to play that role is up to each one alone. Even the child's father cannot teach her how to be a mother. She must figure it out to the best of her ability every step of the way.

That's the short version.

Your subject has only just begun, and you'll watch many more years of this play out now that I've handed you the torch. Here's the thesis statement you must keep as the black thread, the dark cloud that will follow her over the whole thing:

You are ruining your child.

What you must keep pushing for the rest of her days is this: *Whatever you do, it's ruining him.* The food she is choosing and the sleep method. The way she's answering his questions. The times she raises her voice. The ways she tries to discipline him. The times she must miss a game. The fights she has with his father in the boy's presence. The educational path chosen.

None of it is building him into an amazing person; it's all ruining him.

At the forefront of every decision she makes, you must keep this fear that she's going to wreck his life. You'll use what she has heard others say with gleeful jest—"In twenty years your child will be in therapy because of you." She'll live in constant fear that his adulthood will be spent trying to undo all the damage she did while trying her hardest to do her best. Let this be at the forefront of everything—that her best will never be enough. No matter how hard she tries to do it all with excellence and love and sacrifice, she'll ruin him anyway.

Because of *her*, he'll have so many problems that will come out in adulthood; he'll have to sort through and unpack them and talk about them with his friends and with a therapist. This fear terrifies her. It's a powerful angle for your work that I have set up with relentless diligence over the years. The grip on her here is *so* strong, so do not for a moment think about becoming lazy about this, or you will *absolutely* face punishment.

Another ingredient you may splash into this recipe is a looming dread about how much more challenging the future of her motherhood will be than the present already is. She has tucked away many horror stories that other mothers have shared about how much harder motherhood gets as time goes on. "You think motherhood is hard now?" some will ask her. "Just wait until they're teenagers and you have real problems on your hands!" Or, "I would give anything to go back to sleepless nights and changing diapers instead of what I'm dealing with now!" These comments, whether made with seriousness or in jest, are filed away into her "motherhood fears" filing cabinet, and you can utilize them to stir up anxiety about the future as much as possible. They fill her with agitation.

Our Enemy invites her to look forward with joy to the path ahead and the possibilities the future holds for her life with her children. May she never find a way to do so. Your task is to continue filling her with suffocating anxiety about all that is to come as the journey unfolds day by day.

This methodology is twofold. If she keeps fear at the forefront of every decision she makes, every single thing she does will be an arduous process of trying to figure out which choice causes the least amount of damage. When this is the way her decision-making process works at every stage along the journey, she'll have no confidence in her ability to mother.

When this is started from the beginning of a subject's motherhood (which I did with her, as is our protocol), it causes a disconnect between her heart and the part of her brain that knows she was made to be the mother making choices for this specific child. She was chosen by Him for this. Each of her children was given to her with great purpose, not by any sort of accident. But she need not believe this.

The opposite of a confident mother is one who's unsure and afraid. Your work is to *keep* her unsure and afraid under a suffocating umbrella of self-reliance. You want her totally dependent on her own capabilities, swallowed up in the belief that it's all up to her. Who her child becomes depends entirely on her.

This is another tremendous area of pressure we delight in. If, as you carry on in this work, you're as loud and convincing as I have been, you'll see her trying to muscle through every day of the journey with no dependence on our Enemy whatsoever. She'll live in a constant hamster wheel of trying to be her own savior—and she'll wonder with unremitting exasperation why her heart is burnt out beyond her wildest imaginings.

It's as if she's carrying a massive load of bricks, and her sense of self-reliance makes her oblivious to the fact that He is walking right next to her; He's there to carry the load, and there's no sense in going it alone. I want you to continue teaching her, as I have, that going it alone is what makes sense. Because it doesn't.

As for the tools you possess to execute such deceit, her addiction to her screen is a stalwart aid for us, along with second-guessing and overthinking. The incessant stream of other mothers making different choices, discussing how they discipline and so forth, and broadcasting their techniques and ways of operating will have her wondering if the way others do it will be better for a child in the long run. Like drinking from a fire hose, all the different ways she could choose to carry out motherhood as a whole will overwhelm her to a wonderfully effective degree as we move her toward a motherhood of emptiness and sorrow.

Remember that the night's darkness is something you can always use to your great advantage in discouragement and confusion. In the still of the night, when the day's dust has settled and she can think clearly about something for the first time since she awakened in the morning, you want her thinking about all the things she wishes she'd done differently that day. The moments she raised her voice, forgot the appointment, or rejected her child's invitation to play—all this points back to the dark cloud. Every night she will lie there in the dark, telling herself, "I'm messing up every part of this"—and never saying, "I'm doing my best." If this is the case, you've done well.

The days of her offspring's childhood will quickly march on, and she'll be too busy overthinking everything to enjoy most of it. Instead of having space and peace to behold and celebrate who her children are becoming and how her love is flowing through every part of their souls, it will all be marred by fear. She'll be led by fear of ruining it all rather than the joy of trusting in her chosenness by the Enemy for loving her children fully, freely, and authentically.

We lead with fear, never with love. Fear is the banner, forever.

On we go,

Stoneheart

LETTER 24

Whispered with Gusto

Dear Belphegora,

Failure.

Keep that word in the undercurrent of everything she does in her motherhood. Don't be too overt about it—keep it subtle. Remember, you will thrive in the undercurrent. Her life is naturally chaotic, with many tasks to remember and do. If there's a subtle undercurrent from you making her believe she's failing at them all—then *presto.*

As I've shared with you, there's a natural inclination within her to know how to care for her child. She was uniquely chosen for it by our Enemy, but we do what we can to mask this so she second-guesses every decision she makes, and she feels she's failing at everything.

She brings unique strengths to her mothering, but you can steer her to be so focused on the strengths of other mothers that she never discerns any of her own.

The subject's ever-present screens will, once again, aid you in this. She can watch how other mothers are mothering during every second of her day if she so chooses, so in this you guide her toward the belief that the tiny slivers she sees of the lives of other mothers are the full picture. When she sees mothers who seem consistently put together, she'll feel like a bona fide mess. "Hot mess," they call it (and some wear the label like a trophy!).

When she sees other mothers who put together cohesive parties, have a special knack at dressing their children, make fabulous sensory bins, teach their children lessons effortlessly from the Enemy's Book, or masterfully execute crafts in the most creative of ways, she'll wonder why all this seems to come more naturally to other mothers than to her.

When her children misbehave to intense degrees, she'll wonder why she seems to be the only one who is disciplining her children all wrong. She'll wonder why the children of other mothers seem to behave perfectly while hers cannot keep it together—and she'll see this only as a reflection of her deficiencies.

She'll keep wondering why she's the only mother who's failing. She's just not doing something right. She is all imperfections and shortcomings, not strengths and gifts. It's like another dark cloud hanging over her head the livelong day. You take every opportunity you can to whisper it with gusto.

Other mothers are cut out for this. You are not.

I've harped on this over the years. Our subject is totally demoralized by the imperfections in her mothering, and you must continue to press into this, my faithful student. She can't be good at everything, but I've moved her toward the belief that it's indeed possible. So now she believes she isn't capable. When mothers believe they're not capable, they believe they're insufficient in their mothering. This then builds toward the belief that they're simply inadequate as people. An insufficient person is a failure. That's the formula. Formulas are what we do, always. Like the Pythagorean theorem—you know, $a^2 + b^2 = c^2$. It's become routine, boring mathematics for us—but it works on most of them.

Additionally, you want her to continue to struggle under the weight of the incessant stream of advice and tips constantly poured upon her. Many subjects cannot keep their lips closed when it comes to their desire to give advice to mothers who didn't ask for it. Many tips are given by friends, family members, or people in public without reservation or hesitation—some by well-meaning people, some not. The reality of this can begin to feel suffocating.

As her motherhood carries on in the future, this is how you can twist the undercurrent of every piece of unsolicited advice she's given by all who cannot help themselves: You cause her to believe that anyone who gives advice is criticizing her. Each time others offer her advice, you must subtly whisper to her, *You're being criticized!*

This will compound her discouragement and sorrow as she makes every effort to be the best mother she can with all the knowledge she has. If you make the constant avalanche of tips and advice come across like an incessant stream of criticism, it will increase her struggle and belief that she's an ever-failing individual who is just not up to the task.

If she believes she's the only mother struggling, the only one whose capabilities are limited far beyond what's needed, she'll feel isolated and alone. Isolation and loneliness are paramount in this mission.

A world full of insecure, isolated, lonely, demoralized mothers—this has been the Chief's dream all along. We have momentum. We are making it happen, one mother at a time.

Your progress report is due in two months. With your current performance level, know that right now I'd be forced to give you average marks. Do with that what you will.

Talk soon,

Stoneheart

LETTER 25

Field of Dreams?

Dearest student,

All these topics are like onions. The motherhood topic is like one of the heaviest, bulkiest onions in the bin at the grocery store. Allow me to continue peeling back the layers for you. But your subject, not you, is the one who will be crying.

I see you haven't lost any forward motion in getting her to believe she's the only one who's not cut out for this task of mothering. I applaud your boosted efforts here and look forward to seeing it continue. Allow me to further explain the blueprint for the total destruction of mothers.

You've heard the phrase "divide and conquer." This is what we do. Divide them to conquer them—to destroy any possibility for a culture of thriving mothers. Thriving mothers are a gateway to thriving families, so we swing as hard as we can and take as many of them out at the knees as possible.

Mothers in some cultures are far more united, especially when they face terrible sufferings together. While we celebrate things like war or poverty, there's no getting around the fact that suffering sometimes encourages people toward support, love, solidarity, camaraderie. The ease and convenience of modern life in wealthy countries like our subject lives in have come at a price—she and many others find themselves deeply isolated in their comfortable mode of existence. They say it takes a village— there once *was* a village, both literal and figurative, and mothers thrived in that infrastructure. They didn't assess what food other mothers were feeding their children or how they were allowing them to sleep or how they gave birth. There wasn't nearly as much shame and second-guessing. There was an infrastructure of togetherness. Mothers found one another in their mothering.

The Chief began to see this camaraderie as an obstacle to the destruction of the family. So we set out to divide the mothers.

We *have* divided them, and we want to keep dividing them.

We tried a few methods, and the one that worked with the least amount of friction was getting them to place themselves in camps. Organic-only camp. Home-birth camp. Hospital-birth camp. Natural-birth camp. Epidural camp. Co-sleeping camp. Crib-sleeping camp. Sleep-training camp. Sleep-training-is-evil-and-heartless camp. Crunchy-granola camp. Vaccines camp. No-vaccines camp. There are plenty more, but you get the idea.

If they don't feel that they belong in a certain camp, they'll create a new one. They'll make one up that combines a few of the others so they feel, as a mother, that they belong *somewhere*. Scrunchy camp. Silky camp.

They create their camps based on what and how they feed their children, the way they birth, the way they let their children sleep, the way their children are educated, the devices they let their children use or prohibit their children from using, and even what cleaning products they use. Division, division, and more division. We've pitted them against each other so subtly that they cannot even recognize the disdain for mothers who are in camps other than their own. This mentality of conflict and judgment (over opinions, methods, and choices) has made way for a culture of conflict to completely obliterate a culture of unity.

They're lonely now, feeling judged or ready to cast judgment at every turn, wondering which mothers are for them and which are against them.

They can't find one another in their mothering anymore.

They belong to one another, yet they have never felt less like they belong anywhere at all.

You should see the way they tout the rightness of their camps. Some of them champion the superiority of their method-ology as if mothers who choose differently are lacking a brain. Brainless fools, those women in other camps—brainless fools who care less for the well-being of their children. We've weaved the mindset of superiority against the other camps with a calcu-lated and careful effort.

I want to explain how this will affect the coming generations of mothers for the long term. Analogies helped me greatly once I learned about what my predecessors have worked toward with female subjects. This was the plan the Chief set out; imagine the scene with me.

A field full of women—all mothers—and they're all stand-ing in their camps. They stand in separate groups, far apart from one another, divided in this disunity we've sown. A woman who has just found out she's a mother approaches the field. When she was told she'd be coming upon a field of mothers to welcome her into motherhood, she imagined a vast group of women standing together, cheering for her with affection and care. But as she walks into this field, she is stunned and confused to see the women all separated.

Someone walks up to her and says, "Which camp do you wish to be a part of? Do your research carefully, then stand with the group you wish to join. Don't mess this up because it cannot be undone."

She is stunned. Motherhood for her now will be researching all the camps, all the ways that others do things, and she'll let this inform her own decisions and plans for her journey as she gets going. Her introduction to motherhood will not be togetherness and love—it won't be a village of women walking hand in hand in camaraderie. Her introduction will be confusion, horribly conflicting opinions, judgmentalism, discord, and uncertainty about which group will be best for her and her child. What a marvelous and confusing commencement to the undertaking of a lifetime, right? We thrive in this.

When she's researching childbirth, she'll watch women fighting over all these preferences. When she's researching feeding, she'll witness discord from all sides about the right way to feed a child. When she's trying to learn about baby sleep, she'll be so lost in the amount of opinions and ways mothers choose to do it that she'll feel utterly afraid of doing it all wrong and ruining everything (most pointedly, her child).

It will be nearly impossible for her to find any group of mothers who are joined under the banner of motherhood in all the shapes it takes. It's like an awful nightmare for them and a glorious dream for us!

With this as her introduction to it all, she'll feel paralyzed by the fear of judgment for how she mothers. As she talks about the choices she's making, she'll wonder if other mothers are judging her for them. She'll frequently ingest the stream of information from her digital portal and regularly question whether she joined the right camp, always wondering if she's doing the right thing. She'll think of her decisions as permanent. No way to shift to another camp. Like lunch groups in high school—impossible to change.

Isn't it brilliant?

Here's to seeing your
dedication continue to
blossom,

Stoneheart

LETTER 26

Death by a Thousand Quizzes

Dearest Belphegora,

We return now to lessons on productivity and academia. All part of the recipe. You've had a few very unfortunate missed opportunities with her to harp on the productivity memo that You Are What You *Do*. I recommend you fish that letter out of whatever drawer you stuffed it in and revisit that part of my instruction so you continue to work on seizing opportunities rather than foolishly dropping the ball.

And so. Productivity. We've tried to use the methods by which these are emphasized in the culture to our advantage, in order to stifle the feminine spirit and to stuff your subject into a box she was never meant to fit into. Allow me to share a bit of background about the way their society is constructed because this helps instruct you on how I've caused her terrible distress over her path in life.

The female subjects bring both a great depth of heart and great intelligence to the world. But throughout childhood the main focus was the brain. She was made to learn and learn and learn some more. Academia was the heartbeat of life from an early age, and the focus was on how much she could learn and how well she could regurgitate it. There was far less focus on the heart—on feeling—and on the complexity and beauty of the human spirit and how to cultivate and tend to it well for a lifetime.

Six or seven hours every childhood day were spent absorbing information, taking tests, being surprised by pop quizzes and more quizzes, then receiving report cards. Report cards taught the young female subjects with their deep sense of feeling that the heart is of no matter in comparison to the brain.

The six or seven hours of using the brain wasn't enough, however. After the full day of learning, she was made to go home and use her brain further with assigned homework that never seemed to end.

For some of them, cultivation of the heart happened mainly at home in the few hours they had left at the end of the day when all the busywork and assignments and activities had been completed.

Most of life revolved around how to set oneself up for success in life solely by using the brain, not the heart. Most of life revolved around how to get into college, not how to thrive as a human being in a society that can be quite challenging. For the most part, deep feeling was removed from the entire equation. They are all smashed into a one-size-doesn't-actually-fit-all box.

The subjects were expected and pushed to live and move and do—to all do the exact same thing, for the most part—and to do it quite well. Billions of complex individuals all expected and pushed to operate and excel in exactly the same way. What an astonishing framework they set up for themselves!

When the focus is taken away from the heart, the importance of feeling is diminished little by little. The heart's significance becomes only a tangential aside. This has worked in our favor, accelerating our mission to diminish the power of the heart. This entire infrastructure made it difficult for some female subjects— like ours—whose strongest traits had to do with the heart. (The infrastructure didn't align well with many of the strengths of the males either—but that's a separate matter.)

The whole of our subject's journey throughout her childhood and teenage years was spent jumping through the hoops of this infrastructure, which was frustrating for reasons she couldn't articulate. There were few opportunities for daily fortification of the heart and utilization of the gifts of the heart. Therefore, what we want them to believe—that feeling deeply is a weakness—was much easier to plant within them and affects them to a great degree. Even as they move on in years and into the workplace, productivity and intellect will trump the strength the feminine heart brings to any atmosphere, every single time.

As in everything, it's all carefully constructed. When they're young and taught that the brain matters infinitely more than the heart, if they later choose to take a path that has mostly to do with the heart, they'll be made to feel silly. Such endeavors will be seen as wasteful and frivolous.

In my next letter I'll give you further lessons on all the ways our attempts to eliminate the heart have benefitted my mission as a whole with your subject. I'll give you a hint: It involves pressure. What part of our work does not? So very little.

Carry on,

Stoneheart

LETTER 27

The Two R's

My pupil,

As you've gathered by now, one of the greatest assets to achieving the discouragement, sorrow, and emptiness we strive for in our subjects is pressure. Internal pressure, external pressure, the pressure they place upon themselves, and the pressure others place upon them.

We thrive in pressure—it's like a weight our subject has to carry around all day as she goes about her duties. When this is pursued correctly, she feels a weighted burden that consistently pushes her to do a certain thing or strive to be a certain way or grasp at something just out of reach. Pressure has been a key component of my work within her, and it should be in your work as well.

Now, off we travel together into our next lesson. What I wish to share with you today intertwines with our previous correspondence on three pillars: *productivity*, *academia*, and *purpose*.

Within the infrastructure of academia and productivity that has been built up for them from the beginning, there are two *R*'s that define their value. When they're young, it's the report card; when they are older, it's the résumé. An astonishing amount of their life is defined by these two *R*'s.

The crux of today's lesson is an important and loaded word— *career*. A career has everything to do with their working life and achievements as they relate to an ability to earn mammon. It's strongly linked with ability to achieve, to climb a ladder. They often call it a "corporate ladder," but it all has to do with securing a more desirable and impressive position and more mammon as they move upward.

Recall what I've previously mentioned about the focus on intelligence and the insufferable amount of brainwork your subject has endured throughout her life. Interlinked with this pressure to perform in academia is the pressure to set up and achieve a fabulous and impressive career. They weren't all designed for such things, but our work is to have each of our subjects believe that it's one of the highest indicators of how worthy and outstanding she is.

As our subject made her way through her teenage years and into her twenties, the messaging in her academic world was clear: You must have a great sense of ambition. Even if you care nothing about advancing in a career, you ought to pretend you care because it's normal and expected. You must be driven to succeed and achieve in some sort of workplace environment. Life isn't about living; it's about *achieving*. You need to *make something of yourself*, whether you want to or not.

That's it. Life is about *making* something of yourself. This is totally contrary to our Enemy's word that He Himself is in fact the way, the truth, and the life. Oh, the stress as our subject attempts to sift through it all and find out what's actually true!

This leaves many females in quite a pressured lurch. We torment them with this pressure in order to rob them of as much peace, joy, and freedom as possible.

This second *R*—résumé—interlocks delightfully well with how the heart has become an extremely unimportant tangential sidenote in academia for the first years of life. The feminine genius that lies within a woman cannot be captured on the piece of paper they call a résumé. We use this to our advantage to augment the pressure to perform, so our subject feels chained down rather than free to live within the guidance of the way, the truth, and the life.

The résumé is of supreme importance in their twenties, thirties, forties. All that she achieves and accomplishes is for this piece of paper that potential employers judge her by. No heart. No depth. No complexity of personhood. Forbid that there's a few years' gap in it where she stepped out of the workforce to do something other than climb any ladders—*nobody* will want her then! The résumé as a list of achievements is proof of how well or poorly she has been able to make something of herself in her youth and young adulthood.

It's amazing how the stress of it all really wears them down. Comparison here is good. It's easy to get her looking around at other women and the jobs they're securing and the titles bestowed upon them. They look in the mirror and ask themselves, "Is a résumé really all I am?" And the persistent messaging for many of them, as they try to secure a job, is *Yes, you are your résumé.* Once you were your grades; now you are your résumé.

That's it. That's life.

Can you imagine a less fulfilling existence?

The subtlety of our work really comes into play when one of them decides against having a career and chooses to do something significantly less impressive, something more focused on the heart. Let me take you back to when our subject decided she was going to go into "ministry."

She had just paid tens of thousands of mammon to walk across a stage and be handed a piece of paper that represented all her hard work and achievements up until that point. A few months later she received an opportunity to take on a role focused on helping others, a role entirely unrelated to ladder-climbing and involving very little mammon. This is where it was my job to come in strong on the importance of career, to derail her from the path it seemed our Enemy was moving her toward.

What a pathetic and unbelievable waste—a waste of all that you've worked for and achieved! You'll never make something of yourself if you go down this path. You'll waste these important years of your youth. And down the road, if you change your mind and choose to embark on a worthwhile career, you'll be too far behind everyone else to succeed.

Sometimes our female subjects consider changing their trajectory, and they choose life paths that are far removed from what's commonly viewed as a career. Our Enemy moves them toward this, and we're always instructed to come in with great ferocity to derail this inclination. Some of them earn considerable degrees then want to serve the poor. Some receive every cord of graduating achievements and become stay-at-home mothers (which makes it especially easy for us to make them think of their lives as a waste). Some spend a great deal of time studying only to decide to take on roles that have little to do with mammon and much more to do with the heart.

These are other areas where we can receive a helpful boost through innocent bystanders who've subscribed wholeheartedly to the belief that an impressive career is the mark of a great life—and who'll try to steer them away from wasting their lives on nonsense like helping others.

We keep this messaging going throughout the entirety of our subject's life, as much as we can. From her youth, to her young adulthood, to adulthood, and beyond. Life isn't about following the Enemy's voice for your path; it's about achieving great things in the eyes of the world.

Overwhelming pressure, endlessly and always.

Sincerely,

Stoneheart

LETTER 28

The Bus Ride

My dear Belphegora,

We turn now to another facet of your subject's life—another piece to this puzzle of destruction, if you will. Hold on tight and pay attention; there is much I must share with you regarding the topic of external appearances, especially for the female subjects. When your subject was still young, there was a moment when she applied some makeup to her face. She felt positive about her appearance until another subject snidely commented, "Who are you trying to impress?"

You'll be astonished at how easy it is to take something spoken off the cuff by someone and use it as ammunition in her life for years. Our subject internalized this comment while still quite young. She didn't want to attempt to feel good about her appearance because she feared someone would think she was trying to impress a male subject. She understood the message that looking good wasn't something she did for herself but for males—that's it. That's all. Looking good was for others, not for her. She was fourteen at the time.

To put pressure on the need for external beauty from an early age—this is part of the plan. In former days it wasn't this way, but our army came to realize how damaging it can be to push it as early as possible and how this drastically shapes our subjects.

For her, the message throughout society's infrastructure is that as a female, her exterior—not her interior—must impress others. Her interior is of no consequence when we're weighing what matters. If her exterior is not impressive, she must do what she can to make it so. The insecurity of the female subjects and the actions they take because of it actually make much of the work in this area quite effortless on our part.

When she was fifteen, a whole group of young people were on a bus riding back from a retreat. They were talking about an upcoming festival, which the male subjects ask the female subjects to attend alongside them. It's a big to-do, and we stirred up many feelings and insecurities with it. (We also use these festivals as prime opportunities to lead them into great sin, but we can explore this later.) Discussing who they thought would extend an invitation, one subject turned to your subject and said, "You don't need to worry about getting invited. You're ugly."

You're ugly.

The stage was set. I didn't even have to try. Didn't have to figure out some covert way to get her to believe it. Someone said it right to her face.

Jaw on the floor. Imagine my shock and glee.

A fifteen-year-old subject doesn't quickly overcome such a statement. As they seek to understand who they are, what they're told is etched deeply into their psyche and their self-image.

Some are called fat, some ugly, some unlovable, some crazy. It doesn't have to be often; sometimes once is all it takes. One time, one word or sentence, has a lifetime impact on a young heart. Whatever is said, from then on it's all a battle for them against this statement uttered. You utilize it, and utilize it, and utilize it again and again, like a shadow following behind her that simply will not leave. It serves as ammunition for years against her true identity and what the Enemy formed her for—believing and living and breathing in freedom.

Notice what was made clear to her: She wouldn't be noticed by a male subject because her exterior was not up to social standards. As early as possible we drill into the young females that a male subject is a prize you can earn if your exterior is impressive. We ensure that they believe male subjects are looking for females with an impressive exterior, not an impressive interior. There's a certain way one must look to be desirable, to be loved—that's what we keep broadcasting.

Instead of focusing on becoming most fully themselves in their years of education and youth—beautifying their interiors, cultivating their gifts—we move a vast majority of them toward complete obsession with securing the prize of a male subject. If you don't have a male prize, you have nothing.

With careful attention, I taught our subject that the ones who *do* secure the prize are better than the ones who can't or don't. They have more worth, more value. This is a message we try to carry on throughout their lives as long as possible. I told her again and again: *If you cannot secure the prize, something must be wrong with you—very wrong.* Usually it's simple to tie that back to the issue of the exterior.

She is an adult, and even now you'll continue to push the importance of the exterior. Our subject struggles with the fact that putting the exterior together seems to come far more easily to other women than it does to her. It's been dozens of years since the task began, and it will never end. She's the only one who can't figure out how to accomplish it. She looks around to see women who can put together their exterior with such effortlessness. *How do they do it?* She's still unsure and insecure after all these years.

We've also used this prize-related blueprint for the young ones—to loop them into viewing their life as a competition. What does one typically do for a prize? Compete. We can successfully make a competition out of securing the male subjects, and this causes the females to feel constantly threatened by one another. What does a subject do when they feel threatened by something or someone? They cut them down in an attempt to do better or get ahead or get the prize.

When our subject was told on the bus that day that she was ugly, the problem for us came when she began to ask the Enemy for healing from the hurt she had experienced. There wasn't much I could do to stop it (earnest, heartfelt seeking is a powerful force for her). She began to invite the Enemy to speak the truth into her heart and heal her deep insecurities—and I can't stop that either.

In our work we want to restrict them from thinking that healing from anything is possible. Hurts are hurts. They never go away—this is the message. Our work is to get them to believe they're on a never-ending hamster wheel of being ugly, unlovable, crazy, slow, or whatever else they've been told. They're stuck, and it will never be fixed.

Our subject asked for healing, and she received it. This set me back a bit; I spent a few days lamenting the angle I'd lost. But we always find a new one—modus operandi.

Always.

With darkness,

Stoneheart

The Carrot and the Mirror

My cherished learner,

We move on now to lessons about the way your subject views her body. This is essential. Don't allow yourself to be distracted, to doze off, or to daydream about this matter. When any woman hears something repeated often enough in her most impressionable years, she will no doubt begin to believe it's true.

Today's lesson has to do with what they call "body image," the way each of them views their physical being. With heart and soul tucked so deeply inside, all they have the sight to see is the outer part of how they were crafted. Through her many screens, the glossy paper periodicals filled with articles and images, advertisements, and more, the undercurrent here has been subtle and calculated to brew the deepest level of discouragement imaginable.

This is the message: *If your body looked different from how it looks now, everything would be different for you. Everything would be better.*

Remain with me while I unpack several facets here. Allow me to start on the ground floor to explain the foundation of all this, and we'll build up from there (or, more accurately, tear down and destroy).

Here's what it all boils down to: The way their bodies look doesn't impact the world; the way their souls look does. So our primary goal with female subjects is to foster an extreme fixation on the body. If they're hyperfixated on the external, it will absolutely take away energy that could be going toward any focus on the soul.

In the laws of physics the energy has to go somewhere. Her energy and thoughts must go toward *something*. It's best to channel it toward that which will not directly improve the world: relentless stress on the outside to distract any attention from the inside and what matters. Your subject will spend years of her life obsessed with the state of her appearance and entangled in the sin of vanity, rather than focusing on the state of her soul. This is fundamental.

Have you caught on yet to our deep-rooted scheming about how to teach our subjects that there's only one way everything should look, one way everything should go? I almost tire of repeating myself, but understand that their bodies are as unique as their fingerprints, with billions of ways the female body can look. Our goal is to promote another one-size-fits-all approach.

All of them, young and old, are bombarded with messaging every single day. When it comes to self-image, we want that messaging to pointedly declare, *There's an ideal way a body should look—and yours doesn't match the look. Yours will never look this way!*

You should feel sorrowful and dejected and ashamed. I began downloading this message as early as possible into your subject's life.

When this is the constant message in her youth, her internal dialogue begins to build into the infrastructure of her mind. *My whole life would be different if only my hips were narrower. . . . If only I didn't have such an unsightly muffin top. . . . If only my chest was bigger . . . I would be able to achieve the standard of beauty I see. I would feel happy, I would feel free. I would feel like the women I see all over my screens and magazines who are happier than me because they've met the ideal.*

To all this frittering and floundering we respond, *You'll never look like that. What a sad, sad thing for you!*

Standing in front of a mirror, she pulls on all the parts of herself that she finds unsightly, if not horrifying. She stands there, beholding herself, altering her body to try to see a different version of who she could be if she didn't have so many problem areas and facets that need to be fixed. She feels such disgust over her appearance, and this disgust is so overwhelming for her that it completely eliminates the possibility of any gratitude for the fact that her very own face is the image and likeness of the Creator.

The next ingredient in this recipe of sorrow is the belief that with the right amount of work, or the appropriate purchases, she should be able to achieve the standard. When her happiness is linked with her ability to meet the standards of a beautiful exterior and she feels she's failing to meet that ideal, she'll feel sorrow. If she feels sorrow, her proclivity to try to purchase what will help her achieve the standard increases dramatically.

She thinks that meeting the ideal could be just one purchase away, one exercise program away, one diet away. Try and
try again. Like the dangling carrot, the end goal is always just
far enough ahead that she keeps running after it, but she never
seems to get there.

Look around at the copious amounts of mammon they spend
to try to achieve an ideal—when they're already the image and
likeness and all they need to do is take care of the gift they have
received. A tremendous victory for us!

Comparison can be fostered quite well here, throughout her
entire life. When she sees or knows a woman who meets the
standard of how she thinks a body should look, jealousy is step
one. Hand in hand with this jealousy comes our companion,
anger. With jealousy brewing within, she has a greater propensity
to be angry at how our Enemy crafted other females in the ways
she wishes she had been crafted. Angry at Him, angry at them.

The end goal is outright hatred of women who she feels meet
the standard. Seething hatred! I've told you before and I'll tell
you again: A world full of women who hate each other is a world
full of fertile soil for our tactics and operations.

She is the image and likeness—always has been, always
will be.

May she never know it. May she never believe it. May she
never embrace it. May she never live it.

Pressing forward,

Stoneheart

LETTER 30

You'll Never Get It Back (They Stole It All)

Dear Belphegora,

I have witnessed your excellent performance recently in the steady stirring up of our subject's fear of ruining her children. Well done. I feel inclined to share more on the topic of body image with you as we further explore this facet of her existence. Stay with me now.

There's nothing we hate more than the ability to create new life. Neither you nor I can do this. It will begin to frustrate you in ways you cannot yet anticipate (you will see). But take heart. The mission here is to get your subject believing that though her body has grown new life, she must look as if she never did.

Her body image, now that she has borne a child, is a sensitive part of her life. You must understand clearly that our Enemy wants her to not only embrace but also celebrate what her body has done. Your goal is to get her to be ashamed of it.

According to our standard protocol, I encouraged in your subject an inherent proclivity toward sorrow and dismay about the changes that were happening to her. From the very beginning of the process, pregnancy and childbirth gave her marks and scars that cannot be erased or undone. There's nothing she can do to change this, and you want her to believe this is bad.

As her body changes and expands and she packs on the pounds (multiple times over), comparing her experience to that of her husband's is a great cause for discouragement. A dovetail piece of this puzzle is to harp on the idea that the bodily changes she must endure—and which her husband does not—are totally unfair.

Our female subjects joke sometimes: "Next pregnancy, I want to be the husband." He carries on without discomfort, exercising to great intensity, acute exhaustion nowhere to be found, not a shred of nausea in sight. As we've moved our subject properly toward comparison in this area, she's watched her body grow larger while her husband's stayed the same, and she's wept that she's the one who must go through this again. It's *her* plight to endure, not his. Not an honor but a burden. How terribly sorrowful for her!

A hyperfixation on comparison with other mothers will also help you achieve what you aim for most. Any one of them who endures this will look different. They'll carry their baby differently, carry their weight differently. Every one of their bodies is unique, but we want them to think they should all look the same.

When she sees a woman who gave birth when she did, but

who's far smaller and who looks more fit than she herself ever has, you want her to be mortified by her own appearance, disgusted when she looks in the mirror. You take this like a bull by the horns.

I've had much success with this. *Look at her! Look how inferior you are to this type of beauty, to this ease of flawlessly accomplishing perfection in pregnancy and birth. You fat, fat pig. Other women simply have a handle on how to look beautiful again after childbearing—but you do not.*

It's imperative that she continue to believe there's something wrong with her in her lack of ability to regain her former appearance. Something's wrong with her that isn't wrong with other females. This is the message—a subtle, sure, clear undercurrent throughout this entire season of her life.

Listen closely—here we reach the depths of what you'll communicate now and into the future. *The marks and scars are ugly, not beautiful.* When she looks in the mirror, we want her to believe fully and deeply that she has now lost her beauty— she has lost it to the life. Continue to place language before her that makes her believe she didn't just lose her beauty; she lost her body. Emphasize at every turn that her desire is all about going back and nothing about going forward. Use words like *ruined.* Make her desperate for bouncing back, getting her body back, reversing everything. Remember, she must want it to be as though none of it ever happened.

Make her fixation be that something was taken from her— not that a child was entrusted to her. We're weaving this into every aspect of the culture. And it's working.

She cannot ever return to who or how she was, but you want her convinced that she must return to how she once looked—and as speedily as possible. At all costs you continue to make sure she believes motherhood has made her ugly, and there's nothing she can do about it.

At every turn get her focusing on all she has lost, not on all she has gained. Do not relent. Discouragement will remain at the forefront of your mission in her motherhood.

This approach may seem trivial to you now, but you'll soon see how powerful it is, and how it snowballs in ways that will greatly surprise you.

> With a pinch of shame and a
> boatload of pressure,
>
> *Stoneheart*

LETTER 31

Until You're Dead

To my spring chicken,

Today I want to address the elephant in the room. The elephant's *wrinkles*, that is. We're continuing to discuss the external, and today's topic is the biology of aging. No, not internally. (Although they say things get quite creaky and unpredictable in there; it wasn't the original plan, but the Chief slithered in, and here we find ourselves.) Our discussion today involves only the exterior—specifically, the exterior changes that come with having lived a life. We will be continuing to work on your ability to apply pressure that steals any shred of internal peace for her; from my observations of your execution, it seems some things are going in one ear and out the other, and it is time for you to step up before the final decisions are made by the Chief about your future. Let us continue with my agenda.

Step-by-step, day by day, we've wired the infrastructure to slowly condition them to absolutely *despise* aging. Resist it.

Reverse it. Fear it at all costs (and some of those costs will boggle your mind when I get into the numbers).

Here's the main mission: She should be ashamed for looking like she has lived.

She's still young, and the pressure is just firing up, like a car engine starting up on a December morning. I've been working steadily on getting this going with our subject. You want her to feel shame over getting older, shame over the natural progression of life, to convince her that to look like you've lived a life is an embarrassing thing. And that embarrassment will lead to a desire to fix it.

Interestingly, most of our work here has been with our female subjects. With the males, the focus lies more on their hair (but that's outside our discussion here).

Over the coming years you'll keep subtly rewiring her to think she needs to take extreme measures to fix the situation—to fix her face, her body, her sagging, ugly, wrinkling self. After all, people all around her are at war with aging. *Everyone's doing it.* (One of our savviest lines of all time—it has wreaked more havoc on the planet than I could describe to you in a year.) Creams, lotions, dyes, injections, surgeries, cutting apart their faces and bodies—they're all remedies for this particular shame. Buy in, and you won't be embarrassed. Buy in, and you'll be able to look at yourself without feeling sick. Buy in, and you'll look like the women around you—smooth and vibrant and vivacious and so young.

As her youth expires, your subject must purchase it again in any way possible. And there's always a new remedy to try.

This is a delightfully slippery slope we've established. Once they're on the slope, once they've bought in, there's no telling when and where it will end. It usually doesn't. It poses a temporary remedy, but then something else is wrong that needs fixing. Something new comes out that promises to be the solution that none of the prior remedies could offer.

Pervasive sorrow will push her toward believing that she'll always need to look like she's twenty-one. It's the type of shame that just eats away at them. She dumps her mammon into the endeavor and will for years. *You have to put on a different face to be beautiful. Not a brave face—an expensive face.*

This is not what He made her for; it's what we want her to think she's forever made for. She thinks about it more than you could imagine. When she sees current photos of herself, all she sees and laments is the aging woman she beholds, not a woman who's vibrant and living. She wonders if people notice how she's changing. She's embarrassed not only to be seen by others but also to look at herself in a mirror when she's alone. How pitiful! To be embarrassed just by seeing herself—a woman who has lived and laughed and loved.

Here's what's most important. Our subjects grow so obsessed with changing the visible parts of themselves that there's no headspace to reflect on all the ways their aging has changed the invisible parts. See how it works? Our voice that says, *You should be embarrassed of your sagging, wrinkling self* will drown out His voice that tells her, *Look at how far you've come.*

We stir up a constant, pervasive emptiness over our subject's exterior that seems almost hopeless to overcome before she's dead. I have her lamenting now that it will never get better; it will only get worse.

Imagine a world where women were so happy about their aging faces, so happy to have lived well for a good, long time. So happy to have had experiences and beheld sunsets and laughed a great deal. Ugh! I despise the thought of it!

Awaiting your reply,

Stoneheart

Opening Night
at the Gallery

Dearest Belphegora,

Let's now dive a bit further into the topic of identity, so you understand the wider scope of how these subjects choose to understand who they are and how they were made.

I'm going to give you a specific and pointed assignment with your subject; it concerns something for which I haven't been able to crack the code. For me, this challenge has been like holding a slippery tuna freshly caught off the Massachusetts coast—I just haven't been able to get a grip on it, although many of our colleagues have had success here. No matter how I've toiled at it, our subject just doesn't care about something that has swept up so many others.

By our own influence and urging, we got these repugnant ones to come up with systems of numbers and letters by which they define all the inner workings of who they are, as well as labels they use to describe their personalities based on stars and nature and other markers. They assess their hearts, minds, souls, and spirits—their tendencies, the things they enjoy doing and hate doing, how they feel about certain tasks or occurrences, and so on—and they pick a number or some letters or a label that coincides with all these things added together.

There are of course billions of people with trillions of intricacies and complexities in the makeup of who they are. But they think they can fit all that entirely into a set of nine numbers or a handful of categories. Imagine it! Billions of unique people being squeezed into the descriptions of just nine numbers. No, not nine hundred. *Nine!* (Even nine hundred would be preposterously small.) We actually tried to get it down to five, but nine was the best we could do.

It's insane—and we love it. Each of them so unique, thinking they can fit themselves into one of only nine descriptions of humanity. The image and likeness of *Him* reduced to a set of a few numbers! So many of our subjects buy into this and lead with it, whenever and wherever they can, broadcasting who they are by using a number or combination of letters or various other labels.

In some of those pathetic schemes there are just two choices—*two!* Billions of people fitting into two choices—I cackled with glee the first time my own predecessor told me of this. Our surreptitious work has, of course, coincided beautifully with creating a culture of surface-level everything.

We love it when our subjects willingly place themselves in any such box. "I'm a _____," they say. They simplify themselves and how they function to this surface-level assessment that goes hand in hand with that mission of ours to cultivate an aversion to depth. When they're defining themselves by a number or a few letters, there's no depth, no celebration of the complexity of who they are. It completely reduces a person to the depth of a piece of cardboard rather than the depth of the Pacific.

There are many added benefits to our duties from these systems they subscribe to. You'd be shocked by how many of them use these classifications and identifiers as an excuse for poor behavior. "Oh, it's just because I'm a _____," they say. Then they brush it off and conveniently forget trying to become better, because they think this poor behavior is who they are and all they'll ever be. They've defined themselves by it, so it makes sense. Their number is the reason for everything and an excuse whenever it seems to align with a problem or shortcoming or sin. *No need to work on yourself; that's just who you are, and there's nothing you can do about it.* This is the easy route we've conditioned them to take.

The next added benefit I've seen across many subjects is that they use classifications to determine why they don't like someone or get along with them. It's simply because of that person's label. They have a saying about never judging a book by its cover, but they love to judge someone by a number. They write off others before being open to them for even a moment, blinded by the system of judging that the numbers and letters provide. If someone identifies as a certain number, and our subject knows that she tends to butt heads with such people, she may never give that person the opportunity to prove that a friendship with them is possible.

Some of them who have difficulty understanding themselves find these identification systems helpful. They use their number or letter assignment as a compass to help them understand why they are the way they are. For us, the great benefit in this is that they never go first to our Enemy and say, "Help me understand why I am the way I am." They never bother to ask Him, never look to Him for insight, never take the time to dive in deeply with Him to understand their personal intricacies. They never take even a moment to ask their Creator specific questions about His creation.

It's as if one of our subjects went to the opening of an artist's exhibit at a gallery, a splendid night of celebration for the artist's incredible gifts, talents, and vision where all in attendance rejoice over the creative process and what it produced. The artist is right there, with his creations covering the perfectly lit walls. But our subject is walking around asking other guests, "Why was this color chosen here? This one has a captivating texture style—what was the inspiration behind it?"

The artist is there for the asking, but the subject is asking everyone else.

It's the same with this assessments business. I know He would answer all of the subjects' questions if they took the time and space to ask, but they've got numbers and letters and tests and the sun to tell them.

When we can prevent them from reaching any true understanding of themselves, we flatten the depth of who they actually are, leaving them confused and floundering rather than sure and steady.

Time will tell how long we can continue to get them to let all these labels and systems speak to them of their identity. May they perpetually consult everyone except the artist Himself.

Reconnect soon,

Stoneheart

LETTER 33

Hide Away

Dear Belphegora,

To the next step. Brick by brick we go, and I hope you're giving yourself time to understand the importance of each piece of this puzzle on the slippery slope to a devastatingly empty existence for your subject.

Dovetailing well with women's frantic search for identity is the way they've fallen so easily to the messaging that they have something to prove. If I've made certain, for any amount of time, to prevent our subject's inherent understanding of her belovedness, the next step has been to convince her that her life must be spent proving something.

We each have a few main messages that we hammer on with our individual subjects, depending how things have panned out in their unique circumstances. Here are a few examples for you, for reference and scope:

You must prove that you're worthy of love.

You must prove that you're worthy of attention.

You must prove that you're not weak.

You must prove that you're likable.

You must prove that you're lovable.

You must prove that you're good enough.

You must prove your intelligence.

You must prove it's okay for you to take up space in this world.

You must prove that you're important.

You must prove that you have a purpose.

You must prove that you're beautiful.

The act of proving something typically involves a great deal of restless and even obsessive striving. To prove anything at all requires a dedicated effort, and we want each female subject to spend her life in hard labor to prove something instead of resting in her inherent belovedness. When we can get them to hook on to at least one of our messages, letting it affect all that they think, say, and do, it builds seamlessly upon that image of someone in frantic search of their car keys.

Day in and day out, our Enemy speaks to her of the care and purpose with which He fashioned her in her mother's womb. His voice tells her, "All that you truly are is good." It's the never-ending truth of her life, and because we cannot alter this truth in any way whatsoever, our task is to drown out His voice as best we can, however we can. Our task is to let our voices be louder, disruptive, impossible to ignore:

All that you are is off-putting.
All that you are is extreme.
All that you are is unlovable.
All that you are will never be enough.
All that you are is purposeless.
All that you are is difficult.
All that you really are is worthless.

In essence, she's anything other than good. We want her to believe this—deeply.

Allow me to recount a story for you. In college our subject heard from a large group of peers that her presence in social situations was a terrible burden and annoyance to them. She was told by those she trusted and believed were friends that not only was she not liked but she was simply unwelcome and unwanted. Having spent months in daily connection and relationship with these peers, she'd had no clue this was the case and was terribly bewildered. This proved to be a tremendously glorious day for my efforts.

You are not likable. This is what they told her, and she believed it from that day forward.

She went through a few stages following this incident. The first was hiding. She thought, *If my presence isn't welcome, and people are so bothered by it, perhaps hiding is my best response.* So she hid away, quietly accomplishing her daily duties and making certain she didn't cause a stir or bother anyone. In an effort to stand out as little as possible, she wore darker clothes. She simply tried with all her might to fade into the background.

This was another incident (like the one on the bus) requiring little effort from me, and the aftereffects unfolded in a way that was almost too good to be true. Our subject spent the following season downtrodden, sorrowful, and tremendously dejected. As I watched this pan out, I realized the only thing I had to convince her of was that *everyone* believed this about her—that her trying to connect with others was pointless because anybody and everybody would find her bothersome and unwelcome. She was lonely as could be, and I was gleeful as ever in my mission.

But there came a point when she got tired of such feelings of dejectedness. She resolved to make an effort to break free, and it was up to me to make sure this freedom never came. Follow me closely here as I show you how the idea of proving something comes into play for our subjects based on their past experiences and sorrows.

Your subject wanted to move toward the belief that she was likable, acceptable, even lovable—so I moved in to nip this in the bud as quickly as possible. I did it with this messaging:

You think you're likable in any sense of that word? Then prove it!

She then moved slowly out of hiding and into hyperawareness of the impressions she made on others. Constantly striving to prove her likability, she scrutinized her own words and actions as they related to others. It was wonderful to witness the way she overthought every interaction, every word she spoke, every conversation—all with a heightened level of stress. She strived intensely not to be found off-putting by anyone. Driving home from social gatherings, she would replay every word she said, wondering if anyone found her presence as intensely distasteful as some had in the past.

This season went on for far longer than even I had anticipated. The life of abundance she longed for was overshadowed by that one day, that one interaction, for years. I simply kept on with the message that proof of her likability had to be her paramount goal.

However, with an increasing awareness of my work, she began to beg our Enemy for healing. Constantly. Despite doubling down on my efforts, this recourse had occurred to her.

He didn't heal her instantaneously but over time. He allowed her to connect one by one with people who saw and loved her for who she is—people who didn't find her bothersome. Not everyone is everyone's cup of tea; the Enemy helped her find her cup of tea.

So I lost my grip. I lost it slowly, one day at a time, overtaken by the power of His healing—which, when it really comes down to it, I cannot compete with, try though I might. My suggestion to you is that in the coming years (if you are allowed to continue with this assignment upon final Assessment) you work on the angle of convincing her she must prove she is a good mother, just as she had to prove she could be a good, likable person.

And so, *proving yourself*. This is just one example of how effective the mission of trying to get any one of them to prove something can be (at least until the Enemy unfairly intervenes). It can overtake everything. And we let that proving and striving and frittering about go on as long as we can. Sometimes it's a few months, sometimes it's a year.

When all goes according to our plan, it's a lifetime.

Step it up,

Stoneheart

LETTER 34

Walk Right Out

Dear Belphegora,

We move now onto the topic of shame. I've mentioned various facets of utmost importance in our work—and shame is near the top of the list.

Shame is one of the most destructive and debilitating tools in our toolkit for making certain the lives of our subjects are utterly devoid of any sense of grace and forgiveness and goodness. Our goal—at all times and in any way possible—is to keep your subject inside an interior place of great despair and loneliness. It's what we call the house of shame. It's where, if we execute this properly and effectively, she'll lock herself away to hide from herself, from others, and most importantly from Him. It's like a dungeon inside her where we are the guards. History has proved time and time again that we do quite well with dungeons.

Many different areas of her past life have the capacity to move her inside this house. Whether it's something that happened to her, a choice made, a sin committed, a habitual season of sin she found nearly impossible to overcome, or thoughts or feelings she experienced—there are many opportunities to plant a seed of shame. That seed can grow into a massive, out-of-control weed that takes over nearly everything, spilling into every corner of her heart and life.

Understand here that shame is best grown in the dark. Every subject our Enemy has ever created struggles in the dark, and our job is to keep them there. It separates and isolates them from others—which, as we've discussed, is also a powerful part of our modus operandi.

So whether it was the terrible relationship she allowed to carry on for embarrassingly longer than she should have, or her immense struggles in pregnancy, or her ongoing difficulties with friendships, I've been able to cultivate her shame in quite a few instances over the years. Throughout her life, she has locked herself into this house of shame as I've told her carefully that whatever her struggle, it's too shameful to ever be shared with anyone. We can steal days, weeks, months, even years of freedom from her when she's convinced that this interior house of shame is where she belongs.

If at any time we notice a concentrated movement by a subject to step out of the house of shame and move toward the light, we've been given a list of remedial statements designed to keep her there longer:

You shouldn't burden others about this.
You should be able to work it out yourself.

Nobody has time to listen to you.
Sharing this would ruin everything.
You're alone in this.
Your failures and sins make you utterly worthless as a
person.
There's no hope of redemption for you because He can
redeem everything except this.

The last one is a personal favorite.

The more she listens to these, the louder they get and the less she can hear the Enemy's voice that speaks the exact opposite of all I've conjured up. I doggedly work against the truth at the core of who she is—that she was created as a child of light. We don't want her believing this, ever—or else she would walk right out into the light.

We don't want her walking in the light.

Understand that the door to her own house of shame is not locked. She has the freedom to walk out anytime. But the above statements, when utilized at proper moments, can intensify her belief that she's locked in, and there's no way out.

An essential facet to this mission is to counteract any movements toward vulnerability and surrender—with the Enemy or with others. Such movements are essential keys to freedom from the shame we work so hard to perpetuate. Vulnerability and surrender, as I've mentioned with you often, can be quite uncomfortable and even painful—*especially* in regard to their shame. Vulnerability with others she trusts helps her to step out of the house of shame, so it's of great importance to convince her that a trusted person would flee at the speed of sound if she shared what is causing her to feel shame.

So many believe they're locked inside. They allow their shame and woundedness to separate them from others, when the truth is that opening up and sharing with vulnerability could bring them far closer together—and move them far closer to Him. It is of supreme importance to prevent this.

If your subject is open to our Enemy in her shame, what she'll find there is love. Our job is to convince her that she'll find only shock and dismay and disgust. He already knows why she's in the house in the first place. He knows it all. He wants to give her healing and freedom from it.

You want her locked in there forever.

Forever and ever,

Stoneheart

LETTER 35

Unfavorable Hoops

To my devoted successor,

Let's now begin our training on friendship.

Let me paint a picture for you about the way friendship works for most of our subjects. When they're younger, most are openhearted to connection. They connect simply and easily, and they form little bonds here and there over toys and interests and activities.

As they grow, friendships can start to hurt them: times they're excluded, a birthday party invitation never received, moments of openness met with a cold shoulder. Friendship becomes harder—more difficult for some than for others.

Recall my conversations with you about insecurity. Remember that insecurity stirs and builds in each of them, and it can cause them to lash out. When they lash out, they get hurt. When they get hurt, they begin to close up. They begin to be less open to connection. It doesn't come as easily anymore. This is our goal.

There was a pivotal moment that occurred on the playground many years ago when our subject was still young and growing. Some girls had formed a club, an exclusive group, and they held charge tightly over who was admitted. Your subject longed for acceptance into this prestigious group ("popular," they call it), and she asked the leader how she could join. The leader let her know that her ticket into the club was eating a scoop of sand in the sandpit at recess. Shocked and dismayed, she was left to weigh her options: Eat sand and be accepted, or decide against it and be left out. She learned then that while acceptance comes easy for some girls, others had to jump through quite difficult hoops to achieve it. She chose to eat the sand—a bitter experience! And the group had disbanded by the next week. So it goes.

Our goal has been to get her to believe that she is the only one who struggles with friendship. Again, to get her feeling as if she's left alone in a corner for her entire lifetime, while everyone else gets selected for the team, invited to the party, made to feel welcome and seen and loved by other women. We want her believing she alone doesn't belong.

I've stirred up tremendous lament over the years that everyone except her is part of a tight-knit friend group. She alone can't seem to figure out friendship with other women. She alone feels awkward in new situations. She alone watches her screen sadly, where photos fly through of gatherings she wasn't even aware of. She's the only one feeling left out—this is what I've taught her.

Attending a wedding where there were twelve bridesmaids, she wondered how the bride had maintained closeness with so many women over so many years when she herself has made such a mess of that. So often over the course of her life, people she thought were friends just stopped talking to her. One moment things were fine; the next, she's left wondering what she possibly said or did that turned them off so abruptly.

It's important to press this issue into serious overthinking—obsession, if you can. Here are some responses you can continue in this direction:

"Was it something I said?" *Yes, you said something weird that turned her off entirely.*

"Did I come off overeager for friendship?" *Yes, you always seem desperate for friends, especially when coming into contact with likable people.*

"Am I destined to feel left out and lonely forever?" *Yes, you'll never find friendships like other women have.*

She's left with no confidence or hope that deep friendships are something she's worthy of or will achieve. She believes she'll never see a day when she's anything more than simply tolerated by others. Keep her there. *Your friends don't love you; they merely tolerate you. You aren't wanted in friendship; you're pitied in friendship. You're a bother to the people you want to befriend.*

If the messaging here is intense and persistent, she'll never hear His voice telling her that she belongs to Him as well as to certain others, and that sometimes she'll have to seek out where others are. But if she believes belonging is not and has never been for her, she won't seek anything at all. Keep her there.

All this messaging I've provided for her (which you'll continue to provide) makes her attempts at cultivating new friendships extremely challenging. This holds her in a place of loneliness and sorrow. I've slogged away at making certain this insecurity within her goes as deeply as possible and carries on through all the seasons of life.

In singlehood the subjects look for other single female subjects to connect with. In marriage they look for other married friends to connect with. When they bear the small ones, they look to connect with other mothers. It's a natural part of their desire for connection with other female subjects who "get" what they're going through.

If your subject is insecure about friendship—on every step of her life's journey, in every season—her loneliness will be a cloud that follows her. She'll watch other women who stick together over the years, who seem to have figured out some sort of magical formula for how to live in immense vulnerability and connection with each other—something she'll never experience. What sorrow for her! What merriment for us!

True friendship adds a layer of abundance to life; may the insecurity we sow make certain that she never knows the joy of that. Keep on keeping on, to destroy everything.

Final judgment looms ahead,

Stoneheart

LETTER 36

The Loud Drive Home

Dear one,

Allow me to carry on here. Remember, the more closed off our subjects are to one another, the more susceptible they are to our tactics and deceit. Another key component to causing blocks against togetherness in their groups is fear of vulnerability.

When it comes to groups of females where she could thrive in openness, it's key to cause our subject to believe she's the only one with messy insides—deep imperfections, fears, failings. This makes it so easy to keep such things on the surface.

An example for you: Your subject was once at a mothers' group where a speaker—who dove thoughtfully into subjects of deep matter and breadth—intended to provide space for discussion and closeness among members. The groups were provided a list of questions on matters of the heart, but instead of opening in vulnerability, they discussed their individual systems in place for housecleaning. When someone gave even the slightest hint of a reply with any oncoming aroma of depth, someone else would steer the conversation right back to the surface. They avoided any vulnerability and talked instead about logistics, scheduling, and all matters except matters of the heart.

This is a perfect picture of what we envision mothers' groups, or any of their female groups, to be: focused on sharing ideas rather than sharing hearts, like snorkeling on the surface instead of scuba diving in the depths. We keep them talking about trivial matters, and we deepen their great reluctance toward vulnerability.

And, of course, when they're so uncomfortable with depth, they can't move away from the surface, and it will be impossible for them to really know each other and see each other. They're like attendees at a never-ending masquerade ball, diligently wearing their intricate masks so none of the messiness can be seen. Oh, how they want to be seen!

Understand that your subject wants to be seen in the deepest way, but I've carefully instilled a fear within her of this actually occurring. She has concocted a wonderful and believable facade of strength and capability and love of others that has little indication of messiness. There's great fear that if she even cracks the door toward real vulnerability, then her real self—even a mere fraction of it—will be tremendously repulsive to others.

If you're seen for who you really are, people will realize that you're neither lovable nor likable. At any moment when she moves toward vulnerability or openness in any fashion, this is the most effective line to employ. It doesn't have to be loud—subtle will work.

There are times when she'll push past this in an attempt to be vulnerable because as she has grown, she knows her need for it.

She understands her desire for connection, no matter how much she tries to deny it or push it away. If she does push through to allow herself to be known, don't see this as failure. Don't allow this to discourage you in your efforts. What you do at that point is get louder after the vulnerability has taken place.

Perhaps she's driving home from her faith group or a get-together with friends. *You shouldn't have shared so much. You embarrassed yourself. What were you thinking? Now they all think you're so weird! You foolishly made the entire conversation about yourself!* With lines like these, you can move her toward feeling physically sick to her stomach with regret for being so open.

I can only chuckle at all the times this has worked so incredibly well and moved her toward deep overthinking and regret rather than celebration of a positive step of openness. In all things you want her to immediately regret and retract steps that lead her toward the fullness of who she was made to be, not celebrate them. Keep her in the straitjacket of anguish instead of allowing her to dance in freedom.

Let me expand now on the topic of your subject allowing herself to be seen for who she truly is. This message works intricately with the way she views our Enemy.

This is not an easy one, but it's of extreme importance that, in our work with female subjects, we get them to believe that who they most deeply are is repulsive to the Enemy. That their messiness, sin, and shame cause Him to turn His back to them, not turn His face toward them. This is an absolutely necessary tie-in to any life of faith.

You want to be seen by Him, but He doesn't want to see you. You're the problem child. His other children are easy for Him to love, but that's not you.

The Enemy knows her, through and through. Inside and out, He understands and knows the absolute and utter depths of every facet of her heart, every angle of her personality, her strengths and weaknesses. He knows everything she has endured, He knows all she has chosen, He knows every hill and valley she has faced with strength, determination, and all the knowledge she had at the time. She is loved for every part of it. And if you're to stifle her faith, you want her to believe that the Enemy doesn't look at all these things and put forth love; rather, He can't believe what a mess she's made of all He's given to her!

They've all made a mess of it. She'll move away from Him when she believes her mess is the biggest, the most hideous, and entirely unworthy of His love.

Subtly we slither,

Stoneheart

LETTER 37

Never Stop Talking

My dear student,

I've just received word on the date for final judgment for you. We will gather with the Chief for final determination about your future on the 26th of the month at two in the afternoon. Put it in your calendar and give the coming weeks all you've got—your opportunities to lead your subject to despair will expire soon. There will be no more chances to prove yourself capable of staying on this assignment, so wisely commandeer every chance you have now.

Life for subjects involves many questions about how they should live. They have questions about how they should dress, what they should eat, what they should watch, how they should date, how they should discern significant choices, how they should raise their children. They're inherently imbued with a deep longing for a guide to direct them to answers for life's most basic questions as well as other questions of intense depth and pondering. They wonder about the right way to do it all, the best way—and in this wondering and questioning, the inevitable outcome is that they'll consult something or someone for answers. They'll each find a guide to consult at every turn.

Understand that our Enemy *is* the guide. They were created to consult our Enemy for every answer to every question. Omniscient, omnipotent, omnipresent—He has all the answers they'll ever need. He is present in prayer, and she has His Book right there with more answers than can be counted. The trick here is to slowly, surely, steadily move her toward consulting one thing and one thing alone—her screen and its ability to lure her into the abyss. For all of it. Articles, videos, periodicals, podcasts. You want her to believe they have all the knowledge she'll ever need.

You want *these* to be her god.

In recent years this has all been a matter of intensely redirecting her mind toward comparing and consulting what others are doing. Instead of letting her go to the Enemy to ask, "How should I dress?" you want her to ask instead, "How are other women dressing?" and consult her screens. Instead of thinking prayerfully, *What should I watch or not watch? What media should I consume, and what should I avoid?* you want her to ask herself, "What are other women watching?" and consult her handheld portal. Instead of going to Him in deep introspection and openness and asking, "How should I navigate dating?" or "How should I raise my children?" or "What should I do with my life?" you want her to seek such guidance from the Web.

The objective is to move her entirely away from approaching Him for guidance. It's slyly and subtly redirecting her focus to always being curious about what others are doing, and it's subconsciously rewiring her to need an instant answer to everything. Our Enemy doesn't always work in instantaneous ways, but we've conditioned her to need the answer *now*. It's like Pavlov's dog—a question rings out like a bell, and her reflexive response is to consult the god of her portal every single time.

Time and again she finds on her screen a limitless number of subjects sharing a limitless number of opinions on what they believe is the right answer to her questions. She finds an endless stream of content that soon gets her into intense information overload. She seeks answers, and there's always more than one answer to sift through.

All this noise has the power to drown out *His* voice. The screen in the palm of her half-folded hands confuses her and leads her off the path of faith and surety in our Enemy's direction and guidance.

This type of comparison and consultation can also be used marvelously in convincing many of them that poor choices that seem out of alignment with their faith are perfectly normal. They like to use the word "normalize." We've employed their screens to normalize a tremendous array of behaviors and choices that were once seen for what they are—hollow, sinful, and completely in line with our mission.

"What are others doing?" She can find out all day. They'll tell her. They never stop talking, but He never stops waiting. Recall again the brilliant artist in the gallery on opening night. He's there for the asking—but she's asking everyone else.

The 26th at two. Time is ticking.

Yours untruly,

Stoneheart

LETTER 38

I Lost My Cup

Belphegora, my pet,

We've divided the mothers and pitted them against one another, and we will continue to carry on with this mission. Next, I want to continue unpacking the work we've done on motherhood as a whole to make it more chaotic and overwhelming than it has ever been in history.

We thrive in this chaos we've created. The mothers are drowning in it. Have you noticed that they are overextended and overwhelmed to the point that they can't experience peace anymore? It's now nearly impossible for them to mother with a clear mind because of the hurricane of overwhelm that surrounds them. It creates agitation within them—and that's where our work blossoms.

As we've discussed, motherhood was once a simpler endeavor. Our subjects maintained their homes and raised their children. They rarely had to drive anywhere. I want to highlight one of the ways we steadily sneaked in to wreak havoc on their peace.

Activities. The word seems harmless, don't you think? But the distraction of an endless heap of commitments and activities taking them out of the home has overwhelmed them to the extent that they struggle to keep up with anything at all. Motherhood is no longer a simple endeavor; it's a juggling act— like juggling flaming knives on a unicycle.

Mothers go from activity to activity to activity at such an overwrought pace that peace is nowhere to be found. A considerable number of them spend their days in their vehicles, maneuvering from place to place, commitment to commitment. For many of them, their minds are cluttered with trying to keep the schedule straight for the entire family.

The well that they pour from in their mothering is already running dry. Does this kind of life give them anything to pour out? Not really. That's the point.

They don't realize it, but this sense of being overwhelmed that we've stirred up affects not only them but also the young ones. Forever in a rush, the children are raised to know that life is an unrelenting race from this to that without an end in sight. Life is not a slow and beautiful thing; it will always be an overwhelming rush—that's what many of them think.

An unceasing stream of overscheduling and overcommitting has fractured the family in a way that was necessary in our plan for the slow destruction of the family unit. Most of them don't eat together at the table anymore. Frantic and disjointed, they rarely have a day when they have any bandwidth to sit and look at one another, much less talk to one another if they can manage to tear their eyes away from their screens. Their pile of commitments is like a strong wrestler pinning them to the floor and not letting up.

On top of the activities, we make sure there's pressure to do everything well as a mother. They must have perfect seasonal decorations, magical birthday parties, well-dressed children. They must make sure their children have perfect credentials for getting into the best schools, and that each child is excelling in one area at least. It's not okay to let children be carefree—they have to hone special skills.

We make sure the mothers feel pressured to believe this. Their children have to zero in on some talent they're good at as early as possible, and they have to work at it even at the cost of family togetherness and unity. Pressure, pressure, and more pressure.

Some children clearly excel at something early on, so it's easy for us to discourage other mothers who feel their child is so obviously less gifted. *What an embarrassment.* Childhood isn't about excelling in anything at all, but one of our great endeavors is to get these mothers believing just the opposite.

This is regional, by the way. In some regions on the globe, the stronghold against this chaos is quite impenetrable, while other cultures give highest importance to this incessant addiction to activities.

Another key piece to this puzzle, as I've shared with you at length, is the constant electronic connectivity your subject allows to be a part of her life. To repeat, none of them were designed to be as connected in this way as they are, and this can be especially overwhelming for mothers trying not only to raise their young ones but also to get back to every point of connection made to them throughout each day.

When their own mothers had small ones, they could talk to someone over the telephone only if they were at home. Left with only a voicemail to respond to every once in a while, a mother was free to be fully dedicated and present to her young ones and to the responsibilities before her. With all the technological advances they've come up with over time, she now brings connectivity with her wherever she goes. It's now understood by her, and by others, that she's available all day at all times, and she's constantly drowning under a deluge of calls, messages, comments, requests, and digital mail that she can never seem to get out from under.

The stress of trying to get back to everyone proves to be another overwhelming weight. It follows her like a dark cloud. In the middle of the night, while rocking the young one, she suddenly remembers the message she forgot to respond to two weeks ago. Oh, the stress when she realizes she never got back to them! This compounds the guilt she feels for not being all things for all people. She cannot do what everyone needs her to do. You can use even a small moment like this to convince her (especially in the midst of a sleepless season) that she's failing at absolutely everything. The guilt overload stirred up by this constant connectivity works well in our favor as we sculpt a motherhood filled with overwhelming chaos rather than peace and freedom.

This strenuous rat race of overcommitment and intense mayhem has cultivated a generation of burnt-out mothers attempting to pour from empty cups. Some of them don't even know where their cups are; they're just trying frantically to keep up with what everyone is doing. Some do possess their cups and spend every day trying to fill them with perpetual distractions and finite nothingness, as I've discussed with you before. This formulaic destruction brings us intense satisfaction.

Empty cup, empty motherhood, empty life.

On our way now, aren't we?

Stoneheart

LETTER 39

Are You Done Yet?

Faithful Belphegora,

We'll now continue with our lessons on how to steal your subject's peace as she tries to follow Him with all her heart, soul, and strength. I'm going to share with you one of the most intensely distressing angles for this. The principles I describe here can apply more broadly—the principles of comparison, competition, performance, and so forth. But given your subject's stage in life, let's focus on how we can disrupt her specifically in the area of family.

The peace-sucking methodology I am going to share with you works better on some than on others, depending on their upbringing and the messaging they've received about what faithfulness actually looks like on a practical level. She and many others so desire to be faithful, and our job is to convince them that they're following Him all wrong or they're *just* missing the mark in not being faithful enough. Whatever the angle is for each subject, the goal is always the same: stressed instead of surrendered. Always. We want them *stressed* instead of *surrendered*. The execution on this is different with every subject.

The angle here with your subject is an incessant focus on family size.

Whether we're talking about the size of other families, how she perceives the tie between her own personal faithfulness and the size of her family, or how others may judge her family size, this is a multifaceted source of distress that you can continue to employ in the years ahead.

Seems silly, right? They all fear being seen as silly for their own area of distress, so they hold their cards quite close on this, which causes a pervasive sense of loneliness and even despair! Most of them fear that if they openly shared about their struggles and fears in following Him, someone would only look at them and say, "Are you serious? How silly and ridiculous to fret about such a thing."

For our own subject, instead of trusting the plan of the Enemy, her own personal discernment, and the trusted direction of those standing on solid ground, you will want her continually pained by the straitjacket of wondering if she has the correct approach. You want to keep her wondering and second-guessing whether she has embraced the effort of pregnancy and childbearing and child-raising often enough to be seen as faithful and feel faithful within. There's no freedom in such stress—and we don't want her to be free.

There's no shortage of opinions on this subject that she can ingest, many of them shared in groups and on her handheld portal of frivolousness. People put forth not only an incredible number of opinions but also sharp judgments on the topic. These opinions and judgments all work to confuse her and cause her to overthink the issue, and overthinking is an excellent path to great distress rather than great peace.

You must understand a few fundamentals here. There are many different reasons that some women can have more children than others have. Some can bear twelve, some cannot bear any. It is an extremely sensitive, personal facet of their lives, and we utilize this to our advantage as much as possible. We're each ordered to find whatever angle causes the most distress for our subject and harp unrelentingly on it.

The subjects themselves aid us in this area of our work because family size is a constant topic of reflection and discussion for many of them. Newly married subjects are regularly badgered about when they plan to have children. Young mothers are constantly asked how many more children they plan or wish to have. A typical example: One day at the playground, a mother is watching her two young ones play. Another woman there asks her, "So, are you done, or do you think you'll have more?"

I've always been thrilled when I could wield harmless, innocent questions as another source of pressure points on our subject's most vulnerable areas. Unsure of how to respond, the mother feels stress about how her answer will be perceived, what it will say about her. This stress is exactly what we want; this is how we want them to live day in and day out. We want them in constant agitation about the possibility of having to say yes again.

This stress and agitation should also permeate the "faithfulness" question for the subjects. We want every last one of them in constant agitation about the possibility of having to say yes to Him again—or, better yet, drowning in perpetual fear of saying yes to begin with—whether that's a yes to another child or to *any* other aspect of their life in following Him. You can slink in and harp on the message in a variety of ways: *If you get closer to Him, just imagine what He will ask of you. Surely He will ask you to let go of things you love. Surely He will ask you to do very hard things. Is that what you want? Of course not!* We want them terrified to make a conscious act of surrender every day, terrified of being asked to give more than they have or to let go of something they hold dear for the sake of following Him ever more closely.

Understand that when any of them says yes to His invitation, it sets us back. Always. Every time. Sometimes the ramifications for us are disastrous. So we must work to prevent it at all costs by sowing fear. But when they do say yes, and put their trust in Him, our protocol is simply to stir up anxiety about the next yes. We want them perpetually unable to rest in one yes, always terrified or distressed over having to say it again.

Rather than let them rest patiently in the present as the plan for their lives unfolds, we want to keep them always preoccupied with how the plan *might* unfold in the future. *Always stressed about the next yes.* Always keep the focus on the prospect of having to surrender again, on the heartache of saying no to self, never zooming out to see the bigger picture. Elevate this pressure in any way possible. It has worked so well. They look in the mirror and wonder, *Will it ever be enough?*

That's where you take it up a notch. You come in with a sledgehammer to her knees again and again with such intense discouragement that it leaves her almost unable to breathe. *No, it will never be enough! You'll always feel as though you're in a terrible deficit, trying to drag yourself out of a hole like an animal caught in quicksand; you'll always feel that you've fallen short of what true faithfulness looks like. What you give of yourself will never, ever be enough.* Watch how she weeps over it.

Understand also how critical it is to keep her believing there's only one way of perfect faithfulness for a woman. Remember the importance of making her believe that faith is a matter of boxes to check—a list of things she must do and be, as a valiant and dedicated woman of faith, especially in comparison to others. When they come to view faithfulness to their calling as a performance and a to-do list, we can make real progress toward emptiness.

The Enemy's message to her again and again, as He invites her into daily trust, is this: *Be not afraid.*

So as loud as you can, you must interject at every opportunity: *Be afraid. Be very afraid!*

If she isn't praying, the chance of your voice being heard increases significantly. So, as in all things, I cannot possibly harp on it enough: Keep her from prayer. This will keep her gripping tightly to her plans, fears, and worries while you keep her tightly in your grip.

Stressed instead of *surrendered.* Don't you forget it.

Judgment looms.

Stoneheart

LETTER 40

Please

Dear Belphegora,

Every move you make now is more weighty than ever in determining your future—and hers. In my opinion, your future is wildly uncertain, and I have no pulse on what the Chief may be thinking about your performance. Her future is also uncertain from where I stand, as she seems to be slipping out of our grasp ever so slightly with each passing day while I would have expected the opposite. Onward we proceed with handheld instruction; it is abundantly clear you are in need of it.

Today we'll revisit fear, one of our greatest tactics to make sure her life is a tangled mess of woe. I want to unpack for you a specific area of fear we stir up to keep her from being a woman at rest (may she never be so). It's a fear that we keep at the forefront of many of the female subjects' minds, and I toiled long and hard at this over the years when I was assigned to our subject, who now seems to be slipping away from you. I hope you understand how important this fear is to keeping your subject overwhelmed and overextended in every way.

She is to fear—at all times—letting others down. It's imperative for her to believe that she must please everyone. She must aim to never be a source of disappointment to others for failing them in any way. The goal is and will always be to let this fear drive her decisions, interactions, and communication with others—to the point that she completely loses sight of what she herself wants. The pressure this stirs up in her everyday interactions is crippling in many ways.

So many requests are made to her—to help lead an initiative, to volunteer for something, to sign up for something, to fill in for someone, to help someone—the list is long. Slowly and surely over time I watched this become a slew of daily requests for your subject's time, energy, and attention.

All the requests are positive from her viewpoint, although she knows that taking on anything else will only overwhelm her further. And so, over time, all I had to do was sneak in and subtly let fear take the lead: *You cannot disappoint them. They need help! What kind of Christian are you if you ignore others' needs? How will their image of you change if you refuse their requests? No is not an option!*

The most positive result for us in cultivating this fear is that she becomes full of guilt and feels as though she must say yes to everything. "Yes" leads to others being happy with her; "no" leads to others being displeased with her.

And so, through my carefully calculated movements, she

said yes to nearly everything for so long. She never asked the Enemy what she should say yes to and what she should say no to. The seeds of guilt so carefully planted overrode any impulse toward discernment or prayer. Instead, she became fully focused on the idea that she could not let others down!

I watched as this specific fear caused her to overextend herself to the point of madness. It was a tremendous success in the realm of discouragement and deep internal unease, and it manifested in great outward frustration that affected many parts of her life. The pile of responsibilities became crushing. She couldn't keep track of all the things she'd said yes to. She couldn't serve her family well; they simply became additions to the list of people with needs and wants she had to meet—more people she must not disappoint and let down.

When we carefully teach our subjects that it all depends on them, this will move their hearts toward a prideful sense of self-reliance rather than reliance on the Enemy. Your subject will depend upon her own strength, her own capabilities, her own power, and this will lead to the emptiness we seek to achieve within her. She doesn't have limitless capabilities, limitless power, limitless ability to do it all, but we want her to believe she should try to conjure it up (especially since she sees other female subjects who appear so limitless).

This leads to burnout faster than a newspaper in a campfire. Instead of surrendering to her own weakness, admitting her inability to be what she feels everyone needs her to be, and learning the humility that can come with the word "no," she will try, try, and try again to do it all—failing every time.

You know what they say: If at first you don't succeed, fail and fail again.

Talk soon,

Stoneheart

P.S. I'll be arriving to your upcoming Assessment about one hour early so we can discuss your case and do some last-minute preparations. Let me know in your response if that time would be feasible for you.

LETTER 41

The Empty Theater

Belphegora,

As we approach your Assessment, there is not much more I can do but share some final points of strife, which may be useful to you in the event that you do get to continue on in this assignment.

One of the greatest points of pain for your subject in particular is the difficulty she has with self-forgiveness. I began to notice over time her inability to let go of her own failures and shortcomings. This is one place where I am sure you can find additional opportunities to tear her down if you put in the effort.

As with every great deceit, our effort is aided by the seed of truth it contains: She really *has* made a mess of some things. All the subjects do; it's part of their condition. Small mistakes, big mistakes. She's made some serious mistakes in her life so far, and some have hurt others in ways both big and small.

And it has been shockingly simple for me to cause her to hate herself for many of them. It's a powerful thing when she holds grudges and resentment against others; when we can get her to hold grudges and resentment and unforgiveness against *herself*, we can then keep her in a permanent state of internal unrest and self-loathing.

If she stops long enough for self-reflection, she can look back on all the younger versions of herself. It's imperative in your mission ahead—should you be allowed to continue—that you never allow her to rejoice in her growth and to instead fixate on all the things she might have done differently (could have, would have, should have), every step of the way.

You want to guide her toward having no compassion whatsoever toward herself, for what she didn't know, what she chose, or what she didn't do. As we turn up the volume of this message, we can move her toward constantly berating and shaming herself rather than trying to embrace and love all the versions of herself that have gotten her to where she is today.

Here's another analogy to help you understand. Throughout her life the movie of her past will be replaying in her mind. It's as though she's sitting in a gigantic movie theater all alone, with scenes from her past playing in a loop on the screen. As she watches herself through each moment, our hope is for her to be screaming and shouting at all the versions of herself she sees on the screen. Sitting there, desperately frantic about what she cannot change about the past, she witnesses herself in her childhood, throughout high school, in her years of singlehood, in her days of dating, and beyond. She can play back every moment when she could have, would have, should have done something different.

As she watches herself while the movie plays, the alternative response would be for her to deeply desire—in every moment of the loop—to give that version of herself a tenderhearted hug filled with compassion and mercy for who she was then, with gratefulness for how every waking moment has brought her to where she is today.

Your work ahead is to make sure that she continues to live in constant disbelief and anger at her own immaturity and naivete instead of extending grace to herself—the same grace the Enemy gave and loved her with then and continues to pour out upon her in every season of learning, growth, mistakes, and change. He is exceedingly generous with the grace He gives, so we want to make our subject believe that grace is for everyone except her, as hers has surely run out.

We toil for a world full of subjects stuck so deeply in a rut of anger toward themselves that they just cannot seem to move forward.

Here's an additional piece of this pie: She *loathes* the pain she has caused others. Therefore, reminding her of this pain as often as possible is quite a useful strategy. At the drop of a hat she can be reminded of a moment when she made a choice that caused pain to others, causing her to grip tightly onto resentment and disappointment toward herself for what she chose.

I've found that you can hang your subject's regrettable choices and major mistakes over her head to steal an incredible amount of peace from her. I recommend bringing the memories of these choices up at strategic moments, such as when she's trying to fall asleep at night.

I have a whole list of the memories (enclosed with this letter) with dates, times, and detailed explanations of why each point bothers her so much. Our subjects have an interesting phrase for dealing with a painful memory of a past failure. They call it "living it down," for some reason. And so, as much as you can, never let her live it down.

I ran into quite a snag when our subject made the decision to try to free herself from gripping so tightly to self-hatred rather than embracing self-forgiveness for all the messes she has made. She started by reflecting on choices that she made without full understanding of the consequences or scope of what was before her. She started to revisit herself in those moments and forgive herself for her lack of knowledge and experience. Then she began to make a conscious effort to return to those moments and to show mercy to herself for not knowing what she was doing and how it would affect others. Slowly her tight-fisted hold on self-hatred began to loosen.

This was already an emerging problem when you inherited responsibility for this subject. I've greatly lamented seeing her dedication to learning self-forgiveness grow in recent months, which I expected you to handle. And to make matters worse, the Enemy has bolstered her efforts greatly. If you aren't vigilant, there's a chance our work in this area will crumble to pieces—a major set-back after years of successful enforcement. She has developed a great desire to be at peace with herself and with her humanity. That involves many moments of letting go of expecting perfection in herself. If you don't regain your footing, it won't just be me who's displeased—the Chief is beginning to notice this situation.

To further strengthen your efforts, allow me to elaborate on the topic of forgiveness. Vitally important as it is to keep her from forgiving herself, the most fundamental part of our work in this area is making sure she believes that what she has done in her life is unforgivable to our Enemy. With a contrite heart, she has returned often to the Enemy after bouts of sin, some more intense than others. Returning to Him again and again over time has made it difficult for me to crack her belief that He's not only all loving but all forgiving. It's much easier for our subjects to forgive themselves when they are resting in the Enemy's mercy and grace.

As she returns again and again for this reconciliation with the Enemy, our job is to introduce doubt: *You are not truly forgiven*, or *You will never be fully forgiven*, or *Forgiveness is for everyone except you.*

Sowing seeds of doubt about His mercy has always been of extreme importance for us in her journey of faith. When doubt in this area prevails, not only is she incessantly angry with herself for her faults and failures but she believes that He, too, is incessantly angry at her over these things. If she believes her sins are too great and her faults too wide to qualify for the truly immeasurable forgiveness she reads about in the Enemy's Book, it will always be an obstacle to her experiencing total freedom in Him. She may believe that mercy is for others, but we must always lead her into a deep sense of despair that she is the exception.

All He has is love for her. As I told you early in our correspondence, her very identity is *beloved*. Therefore, let the heartbeat of her life be fear that He is angry with her and that true forgiveness is just out of reach.

I'll be on the lookout for your response. I'm eager to hear how things are further progressing as we near your appointment on the hot seat—your Assessment is just around the corner.

Diligently,

Stoneheart

LETTER 42

Parting Ways

Belphegora,

    I did all I could, so I cannot find it in any part of my being to feel sorry for you.

    I shared every ounce of my prowess, all that I have worked on and learned, every last bit of knowledge I have for you to find success and relish the thrill of leading her down the path of destruction as I have. I shared every tip and trick so you could prevent the glory of our Enemy and provide every roadblock possible to the life of abundance promised your subject.

    And you failed. You have embarrassed me to an unspeakable degree, and you have officially been demoted.

    What is there left to say? The greatest annoyance for me is that I will receive a new trainee and must start all over again before I can move forward with my promotion. Indeed, a great tragedy for us both—but much more so for me.

    I received the notes from your Assessment, and the Chief found your greatest failures to be your inability to keep her from seeking a deeper faith and keep her stuck in the Web, glued to her rectangular black hole of distraction and discouragement. When she came to the end of her strength and couldn't carry on in the midst of the trials and suffering, we wanted her to just lie down in despair. Instead, she got on her knees and sought Him in prayer—the very activity I warned you to fight against as a top priority. She kept earnestly seeking His heart, His words in the Enemy's Book, and His direction. But you mismanaged things so messily and did nearly nothing to prevent it.

I blame your failure on a near complete lack of subtlety. She recognizes our tactics more easily than she ever did when she was my responsibility. This does not bode well for our ability to keep her locked in our grasp in the future. How could you let this happen?

Belphegora, I had so much hope for you, and everything was set up for your success. Her addiction to screens should have made it easy to keep her wallowing in distraction, comparison, dissatisfaction, envy, competition, and self-hatred. But your clumsy efforts drove her back toward the Enemy, and as you lost our grip there, so many angles began to crumble.

The Chief also noted your failures in keeping her away from the subjects I mentioned who could help keep her rooted, accountable, and zealous in faith rather than lukewarm. You should not have underestimated the power of community to point subjects toward the Enemy's love for them. Minor failures also included the area of vulnerability and depth prevention. The barriers I'd carefully erected against vulnerability with others and our Enemy have crumbled, which led directly to community with others who would help deepen her faith rather than diminish it. A tremendous failure.

I included the notes from the Assessment along with this letter so you can see the full report and flounder in the regret you rightfully should live with.

What a shame. What a shame, indeed. Back to the beginning I go.

Sincerely,

Stoneheart

Farewell

Dear Reader,

I hope that as you've journeyed through this book, these letters have helped you recognize any areas where you have been chained down and ensnared by the lies of the enemy. I have prayed that God would free you in a new way from any deceptions that have kept you drowning in fear, insecurity, discouragement, sin, or self-hatred. Most of all, I pray that in recognizing the enemy's lies you have been freed to move with even greater fervor toward the God who loves you, and the grace, peace, and mercy that can be found in a life lived through Him, with Him, and in Him.

Perhaps this book has provided fodder for vulnerable conversations with other women in your life, maybe even women you have walked through this book with. Perhaps your priorities have changed after reading. Maybe you have sought forgiveness and healing from sin that has plagued your life for years. Perhaps you have had one or more revelations about harmful ways our culture has formed you. Perhaps you are still working through some of the issues or deep hurts these pages have brought up in your heart and in your memory. (I most certainly had to do this myself; if this is where you find yourself, you have my deep compassion for your journey.)

I pray that you will know *always* that our all-powerful God is with you and for you as you work through it all. I hope we can talk in person one day about what your journey through these pages has been like.

Let me leave you with a prayer and encouragement for your journey, from the depths of my heart to yours:

> *May you go forward, having broken free from every demonic lie that has ensnared you, and run toward Jesus and all the grace available through an abundant life lived in Him.*
>
> *May you always know who you are—beloved.*
>
> *May you always know whose you are—His.*
>
> *May you always know what you were created for—His glory.*
>
> *May you always know what His life, death, and resurrection has made you—free.*

Love,
Emily

Acknowledgments

My heart overflows with gratitude for every single soul who made this possible.

Daniël, you always believed this could come to be and never stopped believing. Thank you for your love.

Mom and Dad, this book would not exist without your selfless love and dedication to raising me in a home and family soaked in faith, hope, and perseverance. Mom, thank you for the unwavering prayer warrior that you are. Dad, thank you for weaving the creation of art into the fabric of my heart and life.

Zion and Jedediah, you light up my life like a Christmas tree in December. Pearl, thank you for writing this with me and for encouraging me with your tiny kicks every step of the way. We truly did this together, and it was sweeter than I will ever be able to describe to have you with me through it all.

Dave—can you believe it? Thank you for taking a chance on me, on this, on all of it. Grateful for you. To my editor, Daniel—you have been a truly marvelous companion on this journey. Thank you for your spectacular work on this project. Thank you to all at Thomas Nelson who dedicated their time and efforts to bringing this to life.

Overwhelming gratitude to the wonderful people in Paris who helped me cross the finish line as I wandered in to write in your cafes and churches and receive your hospitality and kindness. To every one of you incredible women who have allowed me to cheer you on over these many years and who have trusted me to guide you and speak words of encouragement over your life—thank you for walking with me and for cheering me on in surrendering to God's call for my life. Your love and support mean more to me than you will ever know.

To our almighty, unstoppable God—all for Your glory, forever and ever. Amen, hallelujah.

About the Author

Emily Wilson Hussem is a speaker, author, wife, and mother who shares her witness of faith at conferences and events across the globe. She shares on the topics of femininity, faith, dating, motherhood, and relationships, and her books, videos, and talks continue to inspire and encourage women of all ages. Emily lives in Southern California with her husband, Daniël, and their three glorious children, Zion, Jedediah, and Pearl.